APPLYING THE BIBLE TO LIFE

T0357288

MARK

BIBLE STUDY

BUILDING OUR
FAITH ON A STRONG
FOUNDATION

KEVIN HARNEY

BASED ON COMMENTARY FROM

DAVID E. GARLAND

Harper*Christian*
Resources

Applying the Bible to Life Series: Mark Bible Study
© 2025 by Kevin Harney and David E. Garland

Published in Grand Rapids, Michigan, by HarperChristian Resources. HarperChristian Resources is a registered trademark of HarperCollins Christian Publishing, Inc.

Requests for information should be sent to customercare@harpercollins.com.

ISBN 978-0-310-17678-7 (softcover)
ISBN 978-0-310-17680-0 (ebook)

HarperChristian Resources titles may be purchased in bulk for church, business, fundraising, or ministry use. For information, please e-mail ResourceSpecialist@ChurchSource.com.

First Printing March 2025 / Printed in the United States of America

25 26 27 28 29 LBC 5 4 3 2 1

Contents

About the
APPLYING THE BIBLE TO LIFE SERIES

Life transformation... that is the bottom line. When the Holy Spirit spoke through James and said that followers of Christ are not to "merely listen to the word" but actually "do what it says" (1:22), it was a declaration that academic study of the Bible is not the whole story. God desires for us to read the Bible, seek to understand it in both its *original* context and in *today's* culture, and then allow what we have read to propel us deeper into the will and ways of our Creator.

This is the goal of the *Applying the Bible to Life* series. The vision is for you to first dig into high-level scholarship that plumbs the depths of biblical history, culture, language, and theology. But you won't just stop there! Next, you will connect the ancient words of the Bible to eternal truths and see how they carry throughout to our modern world today. Finally, the goal is for you to see those eternal truths of God come alive in every part of your life.

Each of the studies in the series is based on *The NIV Application Commentary*—one of the most dynamic and well-rounded volumes of commentaries available today. The scholars behind each of these works take readers on a round-trip journey first back to biblical times and then forward to our times today. Along the way, they dig into deep theological insights that bridge the ancient biblical text to the modern world with theological and interpretive integrity.

Prompts have been provided in each lesson of the *Applying the Bible to Life* series to help guide your experience. Each lesson begins with a brief introduction that identifies a key theme for that session. You will then read the biblical text you will be studying. (**Note that these are selected texts and not every passage in the book of the Bible that you are studying may be covered.**) Try to read every passage slowly, thoughtfully, and prayerfully.

Each biblical passage is followed by an **Original Meaning** section, drawn from *The NIV Application Commentary,* that will help you understand the author's original intent behind the writing and how the original readers would have interpreted that text. This is followed by the **Past to Present** section, which is intended to help you bridge the gap between the ancient and modern and understand how to apply what you just read to your situation today.

You will find **application and reflection questions** in every lesson to help you in this regard. If you are doing this study on your own, use them for reflection, journaling, and digging deeper into your own growth in faith. If you are walking through this study with a few friends or in a small group, use them for group discussion and interaction.

Finally, at the end of each session is a brief **prayer** prompt. This is designed to be a launchpad into a time of personal prayer around the major theme or themes of the session. Use this prayer as a prompt to help you seek God, gain the understanding that he wants you to have, and discover his power at work in your life.

It will be a great adventure . . . so let's begin!

The Gospel of Mark at a Glance

Author: Although the Gospel does not have an author listed in the text, there is consistent testimony in the early church that John Mark is the author. He was a close associate of Peter, who would have passed on firsthand information about the life and ministry of Jesus.

Date: Many believe the Gospel of Mark was written in the AD 50s or early 60s. Others believe it was inspired and penned later, shortly before the destruction of the temple in AD 70. It is widely accepted by scholars that Mark was the first of the four Gospels to be written.

Setting: Mark likely wrote his Gospel from Rome. The church was facing major crises at the time. Christians had to cope with the death of eyewitnesses, which created the need to conserve the traditions about Jesus. Christians also had to deflect government suspicion of them as a potentially subversive group and defend themselves against religious rivals who could foil the church's growth. Mark's written record of the preaching of Peter thus aided the church's task of proclaiming the gospel throughout the Greco-Roman world.

Focus: The focus of Mark's Gospel is that our faith in Jesus is built on the strong foundation that he is the divine Son of God who came in humility to announce the coming of God's kingdom to our world. Jesus, the Servant King, left the glory of heaven to bring hope, healing, life, truth, and grace to all who accept his message. Mark's Gospel is succinct, unadorned, and vivid. His action is fast-paced in the first half of the book but then slows down in the second half. Mark does this to call our attention to the centrality of the cross for disciples of Jesus. In his Gospel, which can be read aloud in about an hour and a half, we encounter the drama of the unveiling of the Messiah intertwined with the humanity of our Savior.

The Messiah Arrives

Mark 1:1-13, 14-15, 16-45

Writers understand the purpose and the power of *backstory*. It is not enough to just introduce a character into a plot and then carry on from there. No, we want to know what makes that person tick. What happened in the past that shaped his or her nature? What trials has that person had to overcome? What trauma stills lingers that is impacting how he or she thinks and acts?

When this information is missing from a story, we feel a bit short-changed. It is as if the writer didn't care enough about us as readers to include those vital details! This can be our reaction when we read the opening chapter in Mark. The only real backstory we are given about Jesus, the protagonist in the story, is a prophecy in Isaiah about a messenger who will prepare the way for him. (This messenger turns out to be John the Baptizer). Jesus then suddenly appears "from Nazareth in Galilee" on the shores of the Jordan River to be baptized.

We are given nothing about Jesus' lineage. No notes about Jesus' earthly parents. No mention of the magi, or the star in the east, or the mad king Herod. No angels appear, and no shepherds come to where Jesus is born. The question is . . . *why*? Why does Mark leave out these details that other Gospel writers include? This is a question we will examine in this lesson. Mark had a purpose in leaving out these details. In fact, what he leaves out tells us a lot about Jesus' identity.

Mark's Prologue [Mark 1:1–13]

[1] The beginning of the good news about Jesus the Messiah, the Son of God, [2] as it is written in Isaiah the prophet:

> "I will send my messenger ahead of you,
>   who will prepare your way"—
> [3] "a voice of one calling in the wilderness,
> 'Prepare the way for the Lord,
>   make straight paths for him.'"

[4] And so John the Baptist appeared in the wilderness, preaching a baptism of repentance for the forgiveness of sins. [5] The whole Judean countryside and all the people of Jerusalem went out to him. Confessing their sins, they were baptized by him in the Jordan River. [6] John wore clothing made of camel's hair, with a leather belt around his waist, and he ate locusts and wild honey. [7] And this was his message: "After me comes the one more powerful than I, the straps of whose sandals I am not worthy to stoop down and untie. [8] I baptize you with water, but he will baptize you with the Holy Spirit."

[9] At that time Jesus came from Nazareth in Galilee and was baptized by John in the Jordan. [10] Just as Jesus was coming up out of the water, he saw heaven being torn open and the Spirit descending on him like a dove. [11] And a voice came from heaven: "You are my Son, whom I love; with you I am well pleased."

[12] At once the Spirit sent him out into the wilderness [13] and he was in the wilderness forty days, being tempted by Satan. He was with the wild animals, and angels attended him.

Original Meaning

Mark introduces his readers to Jesus, the promised Messiah and Son of God. The first verse serves as the title to the work, informing readers the story he will tell is not a typical one. The remaining verses function as a prologue, through which Mark lets his readers in on certain secrets that will remain hidden to the characters in the drama that follows.

Jesus and John seem to appear out of the blue in Mark's Gospel, but it is clear they arise from the foundation of God's plan for the world. Mark shows their arrival is bound to God's promises in the Old Testament and continue the story of his saving activity. Long before the promise-filled preaching of John the Baptizer, there was the promise-filled preaching of Isaiah.

Mark tells us nothing about Jesus' background, pedigree, or birth. Jesus just appears at the shore of the Jordan River to be baptized by John. Mark says the heavens are "torn open" at the event—a sign that God is about to act (see Ezekiel 1:1). What is opened may be closed, but what is torn cannot return to its former state. The barriers have been removed, and God is now in humanity's midst. We can interpret the voice at the baptism as God's announcement that Jesus has been chosen to rule over his people and that he assumes royal power as king.

The Holy Spirit's descent on Jesus "like a dove" does not induce a state of inner tranquility. Rather, it drives Jesus into the desert and the clutches of Satan for forty days (a biblical round number). The mention of the wild beasts conjures up images of Adam, who also started with the beasts in the garden of Eden (see Genesis 2:19). Satan must now contend with a *new* Adam, who has the power of heaven at his side and angels in his corner.

❖ As you consider the significance of Jesus' identity, what is the significance of God removing the "barriers" between heaven and earth?

Past to Present

When it comes to determining how this passage applies to us in the *present*, we first have to look at what it meant to the original readers in the *past*. We will discover that there are timeless truths that can guide us today, much as they did in the time of the Bible.

The Wilderness

When Mark was written, Christians were facing persecution for their faith. So Mark wrote his Gospel to remind believers of the foundation on which that faith was built, introducing Jesus as the promised "Messiah" and "Son of God." In the opening scene, John the Baptist appears in the wilderness to announce the Messiah's arrival. In Scripture, the "wilderness" was where God led the Israelites during the exodus (see Exodus 13:18), the place they left to enter the Promised Land (see Joshua 3:1), and where God said he would lead his people back to him (see Hosea 2:14). The wilderness was God's landscape for refining his people.

Just like Mark's readers, we need a refined faith built on a solid foundation. We also need to know there will be times when God will lead us into the "wilderness," just as Jesus was led into the wilderness for testing. As we experience situations that challenge and stretch our faith, we will be compelled to seek God in prayer and discover the truths that he reveals to us through his Word. It is in life's wilderness journeys that we discover our relationship with him has deepened and we have grown in our faith.

❖ How do you know your faith is built on a firm foundation? When have others challenged that what you believe about Jesus is true?

_____

_____

_____

_____

❖ In what ways has God led you into the "wilderness"? What did you discover about his nature and character during those moments that strengthened your faith?

_____

_____

_____

_____

Satan's Temptations

Mark reveals no details about Satan's temptations in the wilderness or how Jesus overcame them. His readers would have simply understood that Jesus defeated him decisively, as Satan never reappears again in the story. The appearance of the Son of God is therefore depicted as a direct challenge to Satan's realm. Furthermore, Jesus' divinity is revealed in that he dwelt among "wild animals" without harmful consequences, that he had the power and authority to overcome Satan himself, and that he was attended by angels.

This scene teaches that when Satan attacks us, we can receive "victory through our Lord Jesus Christ" (1 Corinthians 15:57). Everything changed when Jesus entered into our world. Satan's dominion is now under attack, and Jesus holds the power over him. As we follow after him, we witness that power and are able to "fight the good fight of the faith" (1 Timothy 6:12).

❖ The psalmist wrote, "Search me, God, and know my heart" (Psalm 139:23). How has asking God to search your heart helped you identify any areas of sin in your life?

_____

_____

_____

_____

❖ Jesus "was tempted in every way, just as we are—yet he did not sin" (Hebrews 4:15). Jesus conquered sin for each of us. How has Jesus recently shown his power over temptations in your life?

_____

_____

_____

_____

_____

Jesus Announces the Good News [Mark 1:14–15]

14 After John was put in prison, Jesus went into Galilee, proclaiming the good news of God. 15 "The time has come," he said. "The kingdom of God has come near. Repent and believe the good news!"

Original Meaning

Jesus emerges triumphant from his battle against Satan and proclaims "the good news of God" throughout Galilee. This is not revival-type preaching (like John's) but the foundational announcement that God's kingdom has arrived. Jesus' ministry begins when "the time has come" on God's calendar. The time of waiting for God's intervention is over, and all that God had said and done in history is reaching its climax. This emphasizes Jesus' role as the Messiah.

Jesus' proclamation comes with a call to action. In the first-century world, messengers who proclaimed the ascension of a new Roman emperor did so with a command for the population to accept him as their king. In the same way, Jesus' announcement that God's kingdom has arrived on earth comes with a demand: "Repent and believe the good news!" The term repent in the Greek (metanoeite) literally means "to change one's mind."

❖ Why did Jesus' proclamation call for a foundational response to first repent and believe?

_____

_____

_____

_____

_____

Past to Present

Consider what this passage meant to the original readers and how it applies to us today.

In the Fullness of Time

Jesus declared that God's kingdom had arrived, yet believers were still facing problems like sickness, injustice, and Roman occupation. This raised a question: *If God's kingdom was now on earth, why did it seem as if the enemy was winning?* A clue is found in Jesus' statement that "the time has come." Mark does not tell us how to understand God's timeline—he just says Jesus' ministry began when God deemed the time was right. God had a plan, hidden from humans, that was working itself out in spite of the seeming triumph of evil powers. While all is not right with the world, it soon would be.

We find ourselves asking the same question today. If God is truly king, then why does it seem as if Satan is winning? Mark reassures us that God is in control of everything that happens but works in his own time. As Peter wrote, "With the Lord a day is like a thousand years, and a thousand years are like a day" (2 Peter 3:8). Even though we can't always see *how* God is at work, we can trust that he *is* at work. For now, we live in a world where sickness, injustice, and corrupt governments often prevail. But one day, according to God's timing, evil will be defeated (see Revelation 20:10).

❖ What are some situations in your life where it took faith to trust the good news of Jesus? How did you witness God breaking through at times into that situation?

_____

_____

_____

_____

❖ What was a moment where you sensed God was asking you to wait on his timing? What was the hardest part of that waiting?

_____

_____

_____

_____

Scenes from Jesus' Early Ministry [Mark 1:16–45]

16 As Jesus walked beside the Sea of Galilee, he saw Simon and his brother Andrew casting a net into the lake, for they were fishermen. 17 "Come, follow me," Jesus said, "and I will send you out to fish for people." 18 At once they left their nets and followed him.

19 When he had gone a little farther, he saw James son of Zebedee and his brother John in a boat, preparing their nets. 20 Without delay he called them, and they left their father Zebedee in the boat with the hired men and followed him.

21 They went to Capernaum, and when the Sabbath came, Jesus went into the synagogue and began to teach. 22 The people were amazed at his teaching, because he taught them as one who had authority, not as the teachers of the law. 23 Just then a man in their synagogue who was possessed by an impure spirit cried out, 24 "What do you want with us, Jesus of Nazareth? Have you come to destroy us? I know who you are—the Holy One of God!"

[25] "Be quiet!" said Jesus sternly. "Come out of him!" [26] The impure spirit shook the man violently and came out of him with a shriek.

[27] The people were all so amazed that they asked each other, "What is this? A new teaching—and with authority! He even gives orders to impure spirits and they obey him." [28] News about him spread quickly over the whole region of Galilee.

[29] As soon as they left the synagogue, they went with James and John to the home of Simon and Andrew. [30] Simon's mother-in-law was in bed with a fever, and they immediately told Jesus about her. [31] So he went to her, took her hand and helped her up. The fever left her and she began to wait on them.

[32] That evening after sunset the people brought to Jesus all the sick and demon-possessed. [33] The whole town gathered at the door, [34] and Jesus healed many who had various diseases. He also drove out many demons, but he would not let the demons speak because they knew who he was.

[35] Very early in the morning, while it was still dark, Jesus got up, left the house and went off to a solitary place, where he prayed. [36] Simon and his companions went to look for him, [37] and when they found him, they exclaimed: "Everyone is looking for you!"

[38] Jesus replied, "Let us go somewhere else—to the nearby villages—so I can preach there also. That is why I have come." [39] So he traveled throughout Galilee, preaching in their synagogues and driving out demons.

[40] A man with leprosy came to him and begged him on his knees, "If you are willing, you can make me clean."

[41] Jesus was indignant. He reached out his hand and touched the man. "I am willing," he said. "Be clean!" [42] Immediately the leprosy left him and he was cleansed.

[43] Jesus sent him away at once with a strong warning: [44] "See that you don't tell this to anyone. But go, show yourself to the priest and offer the sacrifices that Moses commanded for your cleansing, as a testimony

to them." [45] Instead he went out and began to talk freely, spreading the news. As a result, Jesus could no longer enter a town openly but stayed outside in lonely places. Yet the people still came to him from everywhere.

Original Meaning

Mark follows Jesus' announcement of the good news with five scenes that demonstrate the kingdom of God in motion. In the first scene (verses 16–20), Jesus appears by the Sea of Galilee and calls four fishermen to be his disciples. These men show their "repentance"—their complete change of mind—by dropping their nets to heed Jesus' command.

In the second scene (verses 21–28), Jesus enters the synagogue and amazes the crowd with his teaching. The people recognize that Jesus is not just speaking *for* God or *about* God but with the authority *of* God. This is confirmed when an "impure spirit" in a man interrupts Jesus and identifies him as "the Holy One of God." Jesus does not desire testimony about himself from a demon, so he exerts his authority and commands the spirit to come out of the man.

In the third scene (verses 29–34), Jesus heals Peter's mother-in-law of a fever. At the time, many people viewed fever as a divine chastisement curable only by God's intervention (see Deuteronomy 28:22). In the evening, Jesus continues to exert his divine authority by healing the sick and demon-possessed who come pounding at his door. Jesus again prohibits the demons from speaking so they will not offer testimony about his identity, as in scene two.

In the fourth scene (verses 35–39), Jesus goes to a "solitary place" to pray. The Greek term (*eremon*) is also used for "wilderness" in verse 12, where Jesus battled Satan, and the same dynamic is at work here. Jesus travels to a solitary place to receive God's strength, yet he is tempted to return to Capernaum and there receive the praise of the crowd. Jesus refuses and says he will instead travel throughout Galilee. The good news will not be limited to one place.

In the final scene (verses 39–45), a man with leprosy (which included a number of different skin conditions) begs Jesus for healing. Jesus says to the man, "Be clean!" In the Greek, the verb used is an imperative—a command. Jesus is not simply declaring the man to be clean but is commanding the disease to leave his body, just as he commanded the impure spirit to leave the man in scene two. This again illustrates Jesus' authority as the Son of God.

❖ How do each of these scenes reveal Jesus' authority over everything?

_____

_____

_____

_____

_____

_____

Past to Present

Consider what this passage meant to the original readers and how it applies to us today.

Discipleship

All Jewish rabbis in the first century had disciples. However, it was the *disciple* who chose the rabbi, not the other way around. A disciple chose a rabbi based on his knowledge and credentials. But Jesus chose his own disciples—and in doing so, he did not select from the most socially prominent, the best trained, or even the most religiously devout. Rather, his first picks were from a group of fishermen as they were going about their daily lives.

Jesus still calls people to follow him from all walks of life. He is not looking for those who have a certain number of social media followers, or who have achieved a certain level of status, or even who have the most biblical training. Rather, he is looking for people who will leave everything behind unconditionally to follow wherever he leads. We can all be Jesus' disciples and learn from him if we are willing to allow him to transform our lives.

❖ What comes to mind when you think of being a "disciple" of Jesus? What are some of the things that Jesus called you to leave behind to be his follower?

_____

_____

_____

_____

_____

❖ When are times in your life that you have been tempted to believe that God couldn't use you because of your background or because of something you lacked?

_____

_____

_____

_____

Jesus Has Authority

Jesus, in going to the synagogue to teach, was likely following a custom of the day that allowed recognized visiting teachers to preach at the invitation of its leaders. However, when Jesus began teaching, the people quickly recognized there was something different about him. Jesus first taught with *authority* and then revealed that he had *authority* over demons. He then showed that he had authority over illnesses by healing many who came to him.

There is significance in the order that Mark presents. Jesus *first* called a group of fishermen to follow him and *then* taught and ministered with authority. Those first disciples would have *witnessed* such acts of authority. Later, especially in the book of Acts, we find these disciples then *acting* in Christ's authority. Jesus says to all his disciples, "I have given you authority to trample on snakes and scorpions and to overcome all the power of the enemy" (Luke 10:19). We have access to Jesus' authority to overcome Satan in our own lives.

❖ What are some of the ways that Jesus has made his authority evident in your life?

_____

_____

_____

_____

_____

❖ What are some ways that you have experienced that authority through prayer, ministry, and service in Jesus' name?

_____

_____

_____

_____

_____

The Pitfalls of Pride

Mark reveals that Jesus attained a level of popularity when he began his ministry. People were drawn to his teaching. They were amazed at his authority over demons and his power to heal. Soon, the whole town had "gathered at the door" of his home. This attention could have led Jesus, who was fully human, to become puffed up with pride.

Instead, Jesus *retreated* from the crowds and went to a solitary place to pray. When the disciples found him and said his "fans" were waiting for him, Jesus refused to give in to pride and instead said, "Let us go somewhere else." Jesus understood the pitfalls of pride . . . and so should we. When we are tempted to get puffed up because of human praise, we should instead retreat to our heavenly Father and ask him to be the one who fills our lives.

❖ What are some areas in your life where you feel that you are most susceptible to pride?

_____

_____

_____

_____

_____

❖ What steps could you take to be more like Jesus in how you handle these kinds of situations that could lead you into pride?

_____

_____

_____

_____

_____

Closing Prayer: *Lord Jesus, you are the beloved Son of God. You have defeated evil, and you embrace those who suffer. You have all authority, and you call us to leave things behind in order to follow you. You baptize your followers with the Holy Spirit. Please show us how to follow you. Give us the courage to leave behind whatever we need to leave in order to surrender our lives to you and follow you. In your powerful name I pray, amen.*

Controversy and Conflict

Mark 2:1-12, 13-28; 3:13-35

Imagine, for a moment, that you have been invited to a gathering. You find out that a person whom you don't get along with very well will also be there. Maybe this individual has been critical of you, or holds some kind of grudge against you, or is just generally unpleasant. What will you do? Well, if you are like most people, you might try to come up with an excuse as to why you can't attend. Or, if that is not an option, you will try to avoid that other person.

Most of us don't like conflict. However, the reality is that conflict exists in our world and, try as we might, we can't always avoid it. This is just as true for followers of Jesus as it is for everyone else on earth . . . and perhaps even more so. As we discover in Mark's Gospel, just as Jesus encountered conflict, so those who seek to follow after him will face conflict. This is why we need a strong foundation in our faith—so we will not be shaken when the conflict comes.

Jesus had just been baptized and was beginning his public ministry when the tension began to mount. No less than six times in Mark 2–3, we find various groups from the religious hierarchy pressing back against Jesus' healings, teachings, and presence in their territory. Even Jesus' closest family members began to question him! However, in these tense interactions, we find a model in how he responded that we can follow in our lives.

Conflict Over Forgiveness of Sins [Mark 2:1–12]

[1] A few days later, when Jesus again entered Capernaum, the people heard that he had come home. [2] They gathered in such large numbers that there was no room left, not even outside the door, and he preached the word to them. [3] Some men came, bringing to him a paralyzed man, carried by four of them. [4] Since they could not get him to Jesus because of the crowd, they made an opening in the roof above Jesus by digging through it and then lowered the mat the man was lying on. [5] When Jesus saw their faith, he said to the paralyzed man, "Son, your sins are forgiven."

[6] Now some teachers of the law were sitting there, thinking to themselves, [7] "Why does this fellow talk like that? He's blaspheming! Who can forgive sins but God alone?"

[8] Immediately Jesus knew in his spirit that this was what they were thinking in their hearts, and he said to them, "Why are you thinking these things? [9] Which is easier: to say to this paralyzed man, 'Your sins are forgiven,' or to say, 'Get up, take your mat and walk'? [10] But I want you to know that the Son of Man has authority on earth to forgive sins." So he said to the man, [11] "I tell you, get up, take your mat and go home." [12] He got up, took his mat and walked out in full view of them all. This amazed everyone and they praised God, saying, "We have never seen anything like this!"

Original Meaning

The friends of a paralytic man face a roadblock in getting to Jesus: an impenetrable thicket of people had surrounded the house where he was staying. However, as the story progresses, we find the crowd is only one of the obstacles that needs to be overcome. Another, and certainly greater, obstacle is the suspicious skepticism of the teachers of the law.

Mark reports the silent misgivings of these Jewish religious leaders when they hear Jesus proclaiming that the man's sins have been forgiven. They ask themselves, *What authority does this man have to forgive sins?* For them, such a presumption on Jesus' part is an arrogant affront to the majesty of God, which appropriately can be labeled "blasphemy."

Proof that Jesus speaks for God comes in his response to these teachers' unexpressed censure. He knows in his spirit they are questioning him in their hearts. He skirts the issue of blasphemy with a riddling question of his own, in effect saying, "Which is easier, to make a theological pronouncement about the forgiveness of sins? Or to provide empirical proof that this man's sins have indeed been forgiven by virtue of his ability to get up?"

Jesus commands the paralytic to get up and walk so the religious leaders will know the Son of Man has authority to forgive sins on earth. His pronouncement of forgiveness is not just idle theological prattle! This is quickly made real to the teachers of the law when the man obeys Jesus' command, tucks his mat under his arm, and walks out of the house. Presumably, the crowds make way, and the roof is raised once more in an explosion of glory to God. The people's praise confirms that what Jesus has done is no impiety but reason to glorify God.

❖ What was the religious leaders' complaint against Jesus? How did Jesus respond to them?

Past to Present

Consider what this passage meant to the original readers and how it applies to us today.

Spiritual Blindness

These miracles of Jesus reveal that God is for healing—both physical *and* spiritual. Jesus not only healed the man physically but also healed him spiritually by forgiving his sins. The man had faith that Jesus could heal him, and he acted on that faith by getting up, picking up his mat, and walking out. This is a great lesson for us about the power of faith. However, Mark points out that not everyone present had such faith in Jesus. The teachers of the law rightly pointed out that *God alone forgives sins* and that it is blasphemy for a human to presume to forgive sins.

What they failed to admit about Jesus is what the demons in a previous story readily admitted—that Jesus was "the Holy One of God" (Mark 1:24). The teachers of the law were blind to the fact that the Son of God was in their midst . . . which is why Jesus then demonstrated his authority by physically healing the man. In our own lives, we can likewise get so caught up in rules, regulations, and expectations that we miss the fact that Jesus is in our midst and wants to reveal his power. It is only when we have eyes of faith, like the four friends of the paralyzed man had, that we can truly see what Jesus is doing in our lives.

❖ How have you personally seen God bring healing by his divine touch? How have you seen him bring healing through the wonders of modern medicine?

_____

_____

_____

_____

❖ What are some of the rules, regulations, and expectations you have about Jesus that might be getting in the way of you seeing what he is doing in your life?

_____

_____

_____

_____

_____

_____

Conflict Over Eating with Sinners [Mark 2:13–28]

¹³ Once again Jesus went out beside the lake. A large crowd came to him, and he began to teach them. ¹⁴ As he walked along, he saw Levi son of Alphaeus sitting at the tax collector's booth. "Follow me," Jesus told him, and Levi got up and followed him.

¹⁵ While Jesus was having dinner at Levi's house, many tax collectors and sinners were eating with him and his disciples, for there were many who followed him. ¹⁶ When the teachers of the law who were Pharisees saw him eating with the sinners and tax collectors, they asked his disciples: "Why does he eat with tax collectors and sinners?"

¹⁷ On hearing this, Jesus said to them, "It is not the healthy who need a doctor, but the sick. I have not come to call the righteous, but sinners."

¹⁸ Now John's disciples and the Pharisees were fasting. Some people came and asked Jesus, "How is it that John's disciples and the disciples of the Pharisees are fasting, but yours are not?"

¹⁹ Jesus answered, "How can the guests of the bridegroom fast while he is with them? They cannot, so long as they have him with them. ²⁰ But the time will come when the bridegroom will be taken from them, and on that day they will fast.

²¹ "No one sews a patch of unshrunk cloth on an old garment. Otherwise, the new piece will pull away from the old, making the tear worse.

[22] And no one pours new wine into old wineskins. Otherwise, the wine will burst the skins, and both the wine and the wineskins will be ruined. No, they pour new wine into new wineskins."

[23] One Sabbath Jesus was going through the grainfields, and as his disciples walked along, they began to pick some heads of grain. [24] The Pharisees said to him, "Look, why are they doing what is unlawful on the Sabbath?"

[25] He answered, "Have you never read what David did when he and his companions were hungry and in need? [26] In the days of Abiathar the high priest, he entered the house of God and ate the consecrated bread, which is lawful only for priests to eat. And he also gave some to his companions."

[27] Then he said to them, "The Sabbath was made for man, not man for the Sabbath. [28] So the Son of Man is Lord even of the Sabbath."

Original Meaning

Levi responds to Jesus' call as promptly as the fishermen did. He gets up and follows Jesus, but his obedience marks an even more radical break with his past. The other disciples can always go back to fishing, but not so a tax collector who abandons his post.

The next scene finds Levi along with many other tax collectors and sinners eating at "his house." Mark's original readers would have seen in this act that Jesus does more than merely *preach* repentance to sinners—he also *befriends* them. This display of open acceptance appalls the Pharisees, who would want nothing to do with such people. The Pharisees' dismay prompts Jesus to comment about the sick needing a physician. No physician waits for the sickness to pass before treating the patient. Likewise, Jesus is offering the remedy that vanquishes the illness of these "sinners." Instead of sorting people into classifications (holy and unholy, clean and unclean, righteous and sinner), he gathers them under the wings of God's grace.

The section concludes with a Sabbath controversy. The Pharisees, who function here as a kind of religious police, spot the disciples plucking grain as they saunter through a field. Jesus' response recalls a historic precedent when David took it on himself to violate the law by eating the bread of the Presence (see 1 Samuel 21:6). In that story, the strict regulations were set aside because of the urgency of the situation—David and his men were starving. Jesus' point is that he and his disciples are in an even *greater* situation of urgency than David. They are proclaiming the coming of the kingdom of God to earth!

❖ What three questions is Jesus asked in this section? Who is asking the questions?

_____

_____

_____

_____

_____

Past to Present

Reaching Out to Sinners

In this section, Mark presents God's search for humans—even those the world deems the most unworthy. Many Christians today do not recognize that they harbor the same attitudes as the first-century Pharisees in this story. We sing "amazing grace . . . that saved a wretch like me," but we have in mind only our kind of wretches. It is too amazing for us that the same grace is extended to save those whom we believe truly deserve punishment.

It is one thing to go and witness to these kinds of "wretches." It is quite another to treat them as if they were in some way respectable and acceptable—people whom God loves and invites to his own table. We like to put people into categories so we can distinguish between those we consider to be "righteous" and those whom we deem "unrighteous." Yet what we find in Mark's Gospel is Jesus breaking down such barriers.

In so doing, he also makes it clear that we cannot truly love people if we are unwilling to associate with them.

❖ What are some of the dangers in judging others who are not like you? How do you protect your heart from such attitudes that are contrary to God's Word?

_____

_____

_____

_____

❖ Who might Jesus be calling you to "eat" with today? What are some ways you can create an environment of table fellowship based on Jesus' example?

_____

_____

_____

_____

_____

Set Apart for God

The question the Pharisees posed to Jesus about fasting forces us to question the purposes of our religious rites and observances. Fasting is only meaningful when it arises from concerns so deep that the importance of food pales in comparison, not when it is dictated by a checklist or rule book. All spiritual disciplines that aim at setting ourselves apart from and above others is to be rejected.

This is not to say that God wants us to be the *same* as those in the world. As Paul wrote, "Do not conform to the pattern of this world" (Romans 12:2). Observing a day of worship and rest is one way we distinguish ourselves from the world and give witness to our faith. Instead of heeding the calls to bow down to the gods of materialism or play with our particular pile of recreational toys, we set aside time to worship our God and celebrate our faith.

The observance of days and seasons is not the sole element that distinguishes us from others. Jesus affirms that the Sabbath is for doing *good*. He never criticizes the law that requires the Sabbath to be treated as holy. He simply affirms the Sabbath can become an occasion to do good rather than simply a time to refrain from work. The criterion is mercy, not ritual.

❖ What are some of the religious rites and rituals you observe that are especially meaningful to you? Why do those rites and rituals have such meaning in your life?

_____

_____

_____

_____

❖ If you could design a full twenty-four hours of rest, refreshment, worship, community, and encounter with God for your Sabbath, what would that day look like?

_____

_____

_____

_____

The Shaping of Jesus' Ministry [Mark 3:13-35]

[13] Jesus went up on a mountainside and called to him those he wanted, and they came to him. [14] He appointed twelve that they might be with him and that he might send them out to preach [15] and to have authority to drive out demons. [16] These are the twelve he appointed: Simon (to whom he gave the name Peter), [17] James son of Zebedee and his brother John (to

them he gave the name Boanerges, which means "sons of thunder"), [18] Andrew, Philip, Bartholomew, Matthew, Thomas, James son of Alphaeus, Thaddaeus, Simon the Zealot [19] and Judas Iscariot, who betrayed him.

[20] Then Jesus entered a house, and again a crowd gathered, so that he and his disciples were not even able to eat. [21] When his family heard about this, they went to take charge of him, for they said, "He is out of his mind."

[22] And the teachers of the law who came down from Jerusalem said, "He is possessed by Beelzebul! By the prince of demons he is driving out demons."

[23] So Jesus called them over to him and began to speak to them in parables: "How can Satan drive out Satan? [24] If a kingdom is divided against itself, that kingdom cannot stand. [25] If a house is divided against itself, that house cannot stand. [26] And if Satan opposes himself and is divided, he cannot stand; his end has come. [27] In fact, no one can enter a strong man's house without first tying him up. Then he can plunder the strong man's house. [28] Truly I tell you, people can be forgiven all their sins and every slander they utter, [29] but whoever blasphemes against the Holy Spirit will never be forgiven; they are guilty of an eternal sin."

[30] He said this because they were saying, "He has an impure spirit."

[31] Then Jesus' mother and brothers arrived. Standing outside, they sent someone in to call him. [32] A crowd was sitting around him, and they told him, "Your mother and brothers are outside looking for you."

[33] "Who are my mother and my brothers?" he asked.

[34] Then he looked at those seated in a circle around him and said, "Here are my mother and my brothers! [35] Whoever does God's will is my brother and sister and mother."

Original Meaning

As most of those in the Jewish religious establishment pressed back, got angry, and rejected Jesus, the crowds keep gathering. While all this is swirling around the Lord, he decides it is time to gather a core group of leaders to help him in his rapidly expanding ministry. He goes up a mountainside and invites "those he wanted" to come with him (verse 13). There he selects twelve men to be his disciples. These men will remain with him and help carry the load.

This call from Jesus creates a distinction between those who follow after him to seek healing, those who are caught up in the spectacle of it all, and those who come because they have been summoned by him and given a particular task. Just as the Lord "appointed" Moses and Aaron to lead the Israelites (see 1 Samuel 12:6), and Moses "appointed" able men to lead the people (see Exodus 18:25), so Jesus now "appoints" these twelve men to follow where he leads and share the toil of ministry.

Mark reports two other groups that follow after Jesus. The first is Jesus' own family, who appear to "take charge of him" (verse 21). They are intent on silencing Jesus, presumably with the noble (but misguided) intent of squelching any further unwanted attention from the populace and authorities. The second group has less noble intentions. The teachers of the law desire to defame Jesus and sabotage his movement by claiming "by the prince of demons he is driving out demons" (verse 22). Both groups receive a stunning reproof from Jesus.

❖ Who were some of the different groups seeking after Jesus? What were some things these different groups were saying about him?

Past to Present

The Danger of Labels

Mark continually confronts his readers with the question, "Who is Jesus?" The crowds who flock to him from all over Israel see him as a great teacher and miracle-worker while the teachers of the law see him as an agent of Beelzebul, the prince of demons. His own family sees him as one who is "out of his mind" (verse 21)—something frequently attributed to demon possession. The contrast between these reactions to Jesus forces us to decide who is right. Either Jesus is the Son of God who liberates the possessed, or he is himself possessed and an agent of Satan.

Mark's contention is that Jesus *is* the Son of God. Thus, what these opponents of Jesus were doing—by saying he was possessed by Satan—amounts to blasphemy against the Holy Spirit. Of course, it is easy to criticize the religious leaders for their actions. But we need to consider in what ways *we* are also guilty of blaspheming the Spirit, for such blasphemy can take many subtle forms. It is all too easy for us to fall into the trap of slandering those who belong to Jesus because of something we don't like in them. Putting labels on others—like the religious leaders did to Jesus—makes it simpler for us to view them as something other than God's children.

Ultimately, criticism of others in religious circles stems from several motives: sincere distress over something radically new, genuine alarm over what is perceived to be heresy, a desire to reassure that we belong to the good guys by branding others as the bad guys, or a craven dread of losing power. We must pray for the discernment of the Spirit so that our pride, self-interest, and inflexibility do not cloud our judgment of what the Spirit is doing.

❖ How would you describe the way that people today often put "labels" on one another? When have you been guilty of putting a label on another person?

_____

_____

_____

_____

❖ Why is it so important for followers of Jesus to pray for discernment? When is a specific time that the Holy Spirit gave you discernment in a situation?

_____

_____

_____

_____

_____

_____

_____

_____

_____

_____

The Family of God

Jesus' statement, "Whoever does God's will is my brother and sister and mother" (verse 35), has enormous repercussions for the way we treat others. Early readers would have seen that Jesus' definition of "family" embraces those outside of close blood relations—extending to those united by a common purpose. Jesus' understanding counters the ruinous tribalism and the ethnic strife that rears its ugly head in nations around the world. Our shared commitments to God tie us more closely together than biological kinship!

Jesus' words about God's family are good news for _everyone_ in the church. If we all take seriously Jesus' ideal of what the family represents in God's kingdom, it means that we will seek to create and nurture families that make a place for all who want a relationship with God and with one another. This requires more than sharing a pew on Sunday morning and a fellowship doughnut after the sermon ends. Instead, it means that we allow these persons to become our parents, our children, and our siblings. The church is to take those who know the hurt of the world and bring them into the healing of community acceptance.

❖ Who is a person who has become a true member of your spirit family? How has God used this person in your life to enrich you and deepen your faith?

_____

_____

_____

_____

_____

_____

_____

❖ How might God be using *you* to become a family member to someone who needs a brother or sister, father or mother, or a close family connection? What step can you take toward being a spiritual family member for someone in the coming month?

_____

_____

_____

_____

_____

_____

_____

Closing Prayer: *Jesus, in the midst of tension, plots, and attacks, you continued to love, teach, and serve. When people misunderstood you, you were patient and kind. Teach us to be like you. When relational storms loom on the horizon or settle right over our home (and church home), give us your strength and wisdom to respond like you. Thank you for your example of love in this life. Make us more like you with every passing day. In your glorious name, amen!*

Potent Parables

Mark 4:1-9, 10-20, 21-34

When you are trying to put something together—like a bed or a bookshelf—it can be helpful to have detailed, step-by-step instructions to follow. But often it can be even more helpful to watch a video online of a skilled person actually build the thing that you are trying to put together. The same is true when it comes to learning important truths. This is why teachers, speakers, and pastors often illustrate the points they are trying to make with stories.

Jesus understood this fact about humans. He recognized that simple stories could help his listeners understand the more complex truths that he was trying to communicate. It can even be said that Jesus was the *greatest* storyteller in history, for his teachings have endured for more than two thousand years. The words of Jesus, and the truths he communicated, have touched countless lives, influenced untold numbers of people, transformed cultures, and been repeated in a way like no other teacher in all of human history.

The stories that Jesus told, called "parables," were simple tales involving things the people of his day could understand—a farmer sowing seed, a woman looking for a coin, a fisherman casting a net. Yet beneath the surface, they offered deeper spiritual truths for those (like the disciples) who went in search of them. In the same way, when we slow down, dig in, listen well, and allow our hearts to engage with these parables, we find they have a potency that can transform our hearts and help us establish our faith on a firm foundation.

The Parable of the Sower [Mark 4:1–9]

[1] Again Jesus began to teach by the lake. The crowd that gathered around him was so large that he got into a boat and sat in it out on the lake, while all the people were along the shore at the water's edge. [2] He taught them many things by parables, and in his teaching said: [3] "Listen! A farmer went out to sow his seed. [4] As he was scattering the seed, some fell along the path, and the birds came and ate it up. [5] Some fell on rocky places, where it did not have much soil. It sprang up quickly, because the soil was shallow. [6] But when the sun came up, the plants were scorched, and they withered because they had no root. [7] Other seed fell among thorns, which grew up and choked the plants, so that they did not bear grain. [8] Still other seed fell on good soil. It came up, grew and produced a crop, some multiplying thirty, some sixty, some a hundred times."

[9] Then Jesus said, "Whoever has ears to hear, let them hear."

Original Meaning

As the scene opens, the crowds have become so large that Jesus has to teach from a boat in the Sea of Galilee. Mark relates that Jesus taught in this instance "by parables" (verse 1), which in this case happens to be a parable about his teaching. The story reveals the various ways people will respond to Jesus' words and the impact this will have on them.

The parable itself is about a farmer sowing seed, which would have been a familiar image to Jesus' hearers. Following the normal practice of the day, the farmer would have prepared the field before the seed was sown, and the field would have been continually worked. The seed in this case falls on many different types of "ground," yet even the harvest yield of thirty, sixty, and one hundred hardly represents a spectacular harvest. The hundredfold yield given to Isaac in Genesis 26:12 is the normal blessing that comes to the righteous.

Jesus' parable gives remarkable attention to describing the failure of the seed and the reasons for it. The harvest is therefore not the sole focus of the parable. Rather, the parable places more emphasis on the waste of seed in most places than on the plentiful success in one.

❖ What strikes you about the farmer in this story? What does Jesus say about the different types of soil where the seed fell?

Past to Present

Consider what this passage meant to the original readers and how it applies to us today.

The Nature of Sowing

The parable portrays a farmer who sows with abandon—casting seed on a pathway, rocks, and thorns as well as on good ground. He is cultivating marginal ground and laboring against formidable odds, so the rate of failure is not surprising . . . nor is the report of an average to mediocre yield from the seed even in good soil. Given the nature of the land, the farmer meets with frustration and failure, but in the end, he does receive a reward for his labors.

Jesus implies in the parable that the farmer fully expects to meet with failure and success. Yet Jesus fastens more attention on the reasons for the failure than the reasons for success. Just as the field has different yields, the parable yields a number of points that Mark's original readers would have gleaned, and which we can also glean today.

First, it makes all the difference in the world *who tells this parable* and what our stance is toward that person. The astounding implication, which only a few will see, is that Jesus comes as the end-time sower of God. How we respond to his teaching determines whether we will ultimately be included or excluded in God's eternal kingdom.

Second, the *sower sows liberally*—even in unfruitful ground—in hope of a harvest. Just as God sends rain on the just and the unjust (see Matthew 5:45), so Jesus sows his word on good and bad soil. The parable therefore depicts a prodigal sower who excludes no one on principle. The same must be true when it comes to the way we sow the seed of the gospel.

Third, the parable affirms *the farmer will have a harvest* from good soil. He does not go out to waste seed but to gain a harvest. One can be assured the harvest will come from the response of the good soil. When we sow the seed of the gospel, we may not witness the results. But we can be assured that what we have sown on good soil will reap a harvest.

Finally, the parable makes it clear that *fruit-bearing is an essential mark* of the kingdom of God. The appearance of God's kingdom in Jesus' ministry did not come in one fell swoop. Evil did not vanish straightaway with the coming of Jesus, and people did not universally respond to his message. For this reason, we must persevere in continuing to sow the seed of the gospel, knowing some of it will fall on good soil.

❖ What do you learn from this parable about why people need to hear the message of the gospel? In what ways are you to "sow" that seed so people will encounter it?

_____

_____

_____

_____

_____

❖ What is the promise from God about what will happen when you faithfully share the good news of Jesus? How does this help you know your efforts matter?

_____

_____

_____

_____

_____

The Parable Explained [Mark 4:10–20]

[10] When he was alone, the Twelve and the others around him asked him about the parables. [11] He told them, "The secret of the kingdom of God has been given to you. But to those on the outside everything is said in parables [12] so that,

"'they may be ever seeing but never perceiving,
    and ever hearing but never understanding;
otherwise they might turn and be forgiven!'"

[13] Then Jesus said to them, "Don't you understand this parable? How then will you understand any parable? [14] The farmer sows the word. [15] Some people are like seed along the path, where the word is sown. As soon as they hear it, Satan comes and takes away the word that was sown in them. [16] Others, like seed sown on rocky places, hear the word and at once receive it with joy. [17] But since they have no root, they last only a short time. When trouble or persecution comes because of the word, they quickly fall away. [18] Still others, like seed sown among thorns, hear the word; [19] but the worries of this life, the deceitfulness of wealth and the desires for other things come in and choke the word, making it unfruitful. [20] Others, like seed sown on good soil, hear the word, accept it, and produce a crop—some thirty, some sixty, some a hundred times what was sown."

Original Meaning

The fact the twelve disciples (and others around them) asked Jesus about the parables indicates that there is a separation from those who desire to be on the *inside* and those who choose to remain on the *outside*. The "secret" of God's kingdom is available to all, but only some will seek to find it. Jesus deliberately clouds the truth to keep the outsiders on the outside.

Jesus characterizes the parables as mysteries or secrets, so everyone needs his interpretation to understand them. Note that the phrase "in parables" in verse 11 takes on a different meaning from its use in verse 2. It now means *bewildering puzzles*. Revelation becomes riddles and stumpers to the hardened, shallow, and indifferent mind—and the end result is puzzlement. These people do not suffer from a thick skull but a hardened heart.

God once told the prophet Isaiah to preach in spite of warning him that it would only harden the hearts of the hearers until God carried out his punishment: "Go and tell this people: 'Be ever hearing, but never understanding; be ever seeing, but never perceiving.' Make the heart of this people calloused; make their ears dull and close their eyes. Otherwise they might see with their eyes, hear with their ears, understand with their hearts, and turn and be healed" (Isaiah 6:9–10).

This command brims over with irony and scorn. God called a faithful prophet to preach to faithless people! Jesus' explanation for the parables in verse 12 has the same ironic tenor and can be translated, "So that they may indeed see but not perceive, and may indeed hear but not understand, because the last thing they want is to turn and have their sins forgiven."

Mark's readers would have understood that those who possess the secret of the kingdom can see what others cannot. It was God's plan for Jesus—who sowed the seed—to suffer, die, and rise again to pay the price for humanity's sins. The kingdom of God thus advances not just through miracles but also through suffering and persecution. This would have given the early Christians, who were facing persecution for their beliefs, great hope.

❖ What does this passage imply is the real difference between insiders and outsiders?

_____

_____

_____

_____

_____

_____

Past to Present

Ears to Hear

The context in Mark assumes there can be no understanding without interpretation. However, Mark also reveals that Jesus provides such interpretation for *everyone* who asks. Applying this to our lives today, the only way we can understand the truths or "secrets" of God's kingdom is to ask God to give us new eyes and new ears and transform our being.

If we take no interest or action in learning about the things of God, we will remain in a fog. However, if we seek God for understanding, he leads us along the path of understanding and provides us with spiritual insight. Ultimately, we cannot grasp the mysteries of God through intellectual capacity. Rather, God gives it to those open to the truth.

As disciples of Jesus, we are no different from anyone in needing explanations for the mysteries of God. Yet we are different from outsiders in that we *choose* to come to Jesus for explanations. Having ears to ear, of course, does not mean we know everything. We are wise only in the sense that we have knowledge that will save our lives. Even those close to Jesus can be baffled and deceived and must watch how they listen.

❖ The disciples approached Jesus in private to learn "inside" information about God's kingdom. In what ways do you actively and intentionally do the same?

_____

_____

_____

_____

❖ What are some truths of the kingdom of God that you have heard and are eager to share with others?

_____

_____

_____

Success Comes from God

We can apply the parable to our role as sowers of God's Word. As already mentioned, the sower in the parable does not prejudge the soil. He casts the seeds with abandon, not concerned with whether the soil has potential or not. In the same way, God asks us to sow the seed of the gospel with abandon. It is not about hitting only certain "target" groups.

When we do this faithfully, we must then recognize that the success of what we have sown is completely dependent on God. As sowers of the seed, we can take no credit for any success that comes from our sowing, nor do we need to beat ourselves down for any failure. As the apostle Paul said to one community of believers, "Neither the one who plants nor the one who waters is anything, but only God, who makes things grow. The one who plants and the one who waters have one purpose, and they will each be rewarded according to their own labor" (1 Corinthians 3:7–8). No one can boast about a particularly productive field.

As sowers, we *are* to aim for success—a harvest. But the peril is that we become so consumed with the outward signs of success that we get converts with no deeply rooted system that will support them over the long haul. Rather, we want to encourage those who come to Christ to also become *insiders* (like us) who are motivated and activated to seek out the mysteries of God. We want people to come to Christ for interpretation so their roots will sink in deep. In this way, we help others become true disciples of Jesus.

❖ In what ways might you be tempted to prejudge the people you know? What does this parable say about sharing the gospel regardless of how you think people will receive it?

_____

_____

_____

_____

❖ Why do you think both Jesus and Paul stress that the success of the harvest is not up to you? What perils have you personally seen when you focus on outward success?

_____

_____

_____

_____

_____

Rapid-Fire Parables [Mark 4:21–34]

21 He said to them, "Do you bring in a lamp to put it under a bowl or a bed? Instead, don't you put it on its stand? 22 For whatever is hidden is meant to be disclosed, and whatever is concealed is meant to be brought out into the open. 23 If anyone has ears to hear, let them hear."

24 "Consider carefully what you hear," he continued. "With the measure you use, it will be measured to you—and even more. 25 Whoever has

will be given more; whoever does not have, even what they have will be taken from them."

²⁶ He also said, "This is what the kingdom of God is like. A man scatters seed on the ground. ²⁷ Night and day, whether he sleeps or gets up, the seed sprouts and grows, though he does not know how. ²⁸ All by itself the soil produces grain—first the stalk, then the head, then the full kernel in the head. ²⁹ As soon as the grain is ripe, he puts the sickle to it, because the harvest has come."

³⁰ Again he said, "What shall we say the kingdom of God is like, or what parable shall we use to describe it? ³¹ It is like a mustard seed, which is the smallest of all seeds on earth. ³² Yet when planted, it grows and becomes the largest of all garden plants, with such big branches that the birds can perch in its shade."

³³ With many similar parables Jesus spoke the word to them, as much as they could understand. ³⁴ He did not say anything to them without using a parable. But when he was alone with his own disciples, he explained everything.

Original Meaning

In the parable of the sower, we find Jesus moving slowly. He tells the story with flair and detail. He describes the different kinds of soil and what keeps the bad soil from producing fruit. Mark then provides a brief "insider's look" on parables in general with a connection that stretches all the way back to the prophet Isaiah. Finally, Jesus explains the meaning of the parable of the sower and gives additional insight to the listeners who want to know more.

What comes next is a rapid-fire succession of short stories with little explanation or commentary. Bursts of truth are illustrated with brief and colorful stories that leave the listener to figure out and continue pondering what Jesus is seeking to teach. Yet this is not to say that the passages are unrelated. The next two parables that Mark presents about the parable of the lamp (verses 21–23) and the measure (verses 24–25) complement Jesus' previous explanation of the parables in verses 10–12. They express in parable what Jesus said plainly to the "insiders" when they asked him privately about the parables.

The second pair of parables, the growing seed (verses 26–29) and the mustard seed (verse 30–32), are clearly counterparts to the longer parable of the sower. They complement each other in developing the theme of the "hiddenness" of God's kingdom.

❖ How many parables does Jesus give in verses 21–34? Which of these parables do you see as being especially related to the parable of the sower?

_____

_____

_____

_____

_____

Past to Present

Parable of the Lamp

The parable of the lamp (verses 21–23) affirms that God's purpose is not to shroud the light in darkness but to make it evident to all. When Jesus was speaking to his disciples, his riddling parables would have been mysterious because he had not yet gone to the cross and been resurrected. This "mystery" only became clearer to people after those events occurred. Now, like Mark's original readers, we know the full story of the gospel—the "lamp" shines brightly for us. What had previously been concealed has now been brought into the open. Our mission, likewise, is to reveal that mystery to others who want to know about God's kingdom. We have a truth to tell.

❖ What are some of the ways that God has "mystified" you in the past when it comes to his timing and how has worked in your life?

_____

_____

_____

_____

❖ What are some of the truths of God that seem to be hidden to people you know? What can you do to reveal God's truth to them?

_____

_____

_____

_____

Parable of the Growing Seed

In this parable (verses 26–29), the farmer has no idea how the seed grows. He just scatters the seed on the ground. The seed holds within itself the secret of its growth, and the earth is said to produce "all by itself" (verse 28). This sequence also assumes that whatever has transpired underground will become visible. What does this mean for us? God's purposes will be fulfilled in _God's_ way. He entrusts the secrets of those purposes only to those who are willing to trust him despite unpromising appearances. Our job, once again, is to sow the seed and trust that the one who created the seed will cause it to grow.

❖ There is a certain measure of "not knowing" when you follow after God. Why is it important for you to embrace the fact you won't always have the answers?

_____

_____

_____

_____

❖ What are some areas in your life that you feel God is "growing" right now? While you can't know everything about his work, what would you like him to reveal to you today?

_____

_____

_____

_____

_____

_____

Parable of the Mustard Seed

One could dismiss the microscopic mustard seed that is the subject of Jesus' next parable (verses 30–32) as something inconsequential. However, it has a power within itself to evolve into something that cannot be ignored and that eventually attracts the birds of heaven. The same thing, Jesus implies, is true of the kingdom of God. It is already present in his work, but it remains concealed and modest. Many would never guess this inconspicuous presence manifests God's power and dominion that will reach out to all the nations.

The imagery of the parable of the mustard seed warns us against identifying the kingdom of God with our own human aspirations. Jesus' picture suggests the kingdom of God—even though it is growing and flourishing—may continue to look like a failure. The tiniest of seeds becomes the greatest of all shrubs . . . but a shrub is still a shrub. God's kingdom will not fit our expectations or specifications. It comes incognito, and up to the very end, we can only trust that Jesus' movement is God's work, when all things will finally be revealed.

The parable of the mustard seed reiterates what our role is in God's growing process. First, we receive the message of the gospel from Jesus, the sower. Next, we become sowers of the gospel ourselves, spreading the seed far and wide wherever we go. We do not worry about the type of soil where the seed falls but trust God to reap his harvest. We also do not concern ourselves with outward signs of whether anything is growing or what it will look like in the end. We leave all of that portion of the process up to our Creator and Lord.

❖ When has God taken something that once seemed small and insignificant in your life (like a mustard seed) and made it grow into something grand and profound?

_____

_____

_____

_____

_____

❖ What areas of your life have you been "clinging" to that you need to fully release to God? Where do you need to have greater trust that God is growing something good?

_____

_____

_____

_____

_____

_____

Closing Prayer: God of creation, teach me patience as I await the unfolding of your plan in this world. Let your kingdom grow in my heart and home. Let me be a faithful sower of your truth in this world, leaving the result of the harvest to you. Give me patience in the waiting and eyes to see the signs of your kingdom coming on earth as it is in heaven. Amen.

Lord of All

Mark 4:35-41; 5:1-20, 21-43

Even the brightest human minds cannot fully comprehend the universe. Scientists, artists, philosophers, teachers, musicians, and poets touch only the hem of the garment of this universe. Immense. Awe-inspiring. Mysterious. Infinite. To read any of the four Gospels (Matthew, Mark, Luke, and John) is to get a glimpse into heaven and the glory of God.

It is through these glimpses that our faith in Jesus as the Lord of the universe is built and strengthened. Jesus was Emmanuel, God with us (see Matthew 1:23). The author of Hebrews states that Jesus is the fullness of the very substance of the Father and perfectly reflects the being of God. It is Jesus who sustains all things by his word (see Hebrews 1:2-3). When we read the Gospel of Mark, we see God on the move, in flesh, in glory.

Yes, the Bible is clear that when Jesus left the glory of heaven and took on human flesh, something was emptied and set aside (see Philippians 2:6-7). But to see Jesus is to see perfect divinity. This is why Jesus told his disciple Philip, "Anyone who has seen me has seen the Father" (John 14:9). In this section of Mark, we see the veil between heaven and earth pulled back and realize that Jesus is truly Lord of creation—and everything in it.

Lord of Creation [Mark 4:35-41]

³⁵ That day when evening came, he said to his disciples, "Let us go over to the other side." ³⁶ Leaving the crowd behind, they took him along, just as he was, in the boat. There were also other boats with him. ³⁷ A furious squall came up, and the waves broke over the boat, so that it was nearly swamped. ³⁸ Jesus was in the stern, sleeping on a cushion. The disciples woke him and said to him, "Teacher, don't you care if we drown?"

³⁹ He got up, rebuked the wind and said to the waves, "Quiet! Be still!" Then the wind died down and it was completely calm.

⁴⁰ He said to his disciples, "Why are you so afraid? Do you still have no faith?"

⁴¹ They were terrified and asked each other, "Who is this? Even the wind and the waves obey him!"

Original Meaning

Jesus urges his disciples to set sail for the other side of the lake. Obedience to this command requires them to leave the crowd and join Jesus in the boat. The "fishermen" disciples presumably take the lead in this regard, because they are the expert mariners. Ironically, they are the ones terrified by the unexpected storm while Jesus sleeps serenely.

It is easy to imagine how, at the end of a long day preaching to hardened hearts, Jesus was physically exhausted. Those attuned to Scripture, however, catch a deeper significance behind his peaceful repose. Jesus' sleep in the midst of a building and then raging storm that churns the sea all around him and fills the boat with water is a sign of his trust in God. It stands in stark contrast to the terror of the disciples.

The disciples do not interpret his untroubled sleep as a sign they can be untroubled as well. They don't see Jesus' peaceful slumber as evidence of his trust in God that will also ensure their welfare. Rather, they regard it as a token of Jesus' indifference to their safety in their hour of need. They awaken Jesus with an indignant wail of complaint, as if he were in some way responsible for their plight. Jesus' rest is another token of his divine sovereignty the disciples do not yet recognize, and the formidable power of the tempest is promptly overcome when he arises and speaks. Jesus answers their anxious cries by rebuking the wind with a word.

After calming the sea, Jesus then turns to rebuke the *disciples* for their hysteria. In this we find that faith is clearly not something that is inborn. It can ebb and flow, depending on circumstances, and is most likely to fizzle in situations of danger. The fear of the disciples, however, does not alleviate after the storm quiets. Instead, it shifts to the person with them in the boat, who has just shown his divine control over the sea. The disciples' awe is appropriate, but they still have only the vaguest inkling of who this man is in their midst.

❖ What was the disciples' reaction to the storm? What was Jesus' reaction to it?

Past to Present

Consider what this passage meant to the original readers and how it applies to us today.

Courage in the Calm

In Mark's Gospel, the "nature miracles" like the calming of the storm in this passage offer profound clues for the disciples to learn Jesus' full identity as the Son of God. Their willingness to follow after Jesus wherever he goes and their inquisitiveness regarding the meaning of the parables shows their openness to new revelation. Now, this miracle of the calming of the sea will point the disciples further along the road of recognizing the truth about Jesus.

Mark's readers would have understood the dangers of being on the Sea of Galilee during a storm. They could empathize with the fear the disciples were feeling. What Mark reveals in this passage is that Jesus is lord over the storms of life—and, because this is true, we can "sleep soundly," knowing that God is in control over all.

Of course, we can easily claim to possess such courage when everything is calm. We can readily have faith in God's deliverance when we do not sense any urgent need to be delivered. However, when we come under extreme pressure, the courage and assurance that Jesus cares for his own, let alone preserves them from ultimate danger, can fade fast. What we need to do in these situations is learn to trust in the one who can rebuke the wind and the waves.

❖ What are some ways that Jesus has revealed in your life that he is Lord over all?

_____

_____

_____

_____

❖ When was a time that Jesus showed up during a hard and confusing season of your life? How did your faith grow through the turmoil you faced?

_____

_____

_____

_____

_____

Deliverance Through the Storms

Reading this account of the storm in Mark's Gospel helps us recognize we must trust in a Savior who does not deliver us *from* storms but *through* storms. Jesus didn't tell his disciples to get out of the boat because he knew a storm was brewing. Rather, he got in the boat with them as they sailed out across the lake. He was there with them in the boat as the water rushed over the sides, but he didn't react to it as they did.

Our faith in Jesus is not a promised refuge from the uncertainties and insecurities of the world. The truth is that there are *no* safe places in life. We can only find security with Jesus and a serenity that this world does not know and cannot give. We can trust that Jesus has beaten down the savage storms and there is no reason to fear anything this life can bring (see Romans 8:31–39). Our role is to get into the boat and trust Jesus to carry us to the other side.

❖ How has Jesus been with you during times of pain, loss, or struggle? What were ways that God delivered and protected you even in the middle of those challenges?

_____

_____

_____

_____

❖ If the Lord always took away the storms of life rather than went through them with you, what learning and growth might you miss out on receiving?

_____

_____

_____

_____

Lord of the Spiritual World [Mark 5:1–20]

¹ They went across the lake to the region of the Gerasenes. ² When Jesus got out of the boat, a man with an impure spirit came from the tombs to meet him. ³ This man lived in the tombs, and no one could bind him anymore, not even with a chain. ⁴ For he had often been chained hand and foot, but he tore the chains apart and broke the irons on his feet. No one was strong enough to subdue him. ⁵ Night and day among the tombs and in the hills he would cry out and cut himself with stones.

⁶ When he saw Jesus from a distance, he ran and fell on his knees in front of him. ⁷ He shouted at the top of his voice, "What do you want with me, Jesus, Son of the Most High God? In God's name don't torture me!" ⁸ For Jesus had said to him, "Come out of this man, you impure spirit!"

⁹ Then Jesus asked him, "What is your name?"

"My name is Legion," he replied, "for we are many." ¹⁰ And he begged Jesus again and again not to send them out of the area.

¹¹ A large herd of pigs was feeding on the nearby hillside. ¹² The demons begged Jesus, "Send us among the pigs; allow us to go into them." ¹³ He gave them permission, and the impure spirits came out and went into the pigs. The herd, about two thousand in number, rushed down the steep bank into the lake and were drowned.

¹⁴ Those tending the pigs ran off and reported this in the town and countryside, and the people went out to see what had happened. ¹⁵ When they came to Jesus, they saw the man who had been possessed by the legion of demons, sitting there, dressed and in his right mind; and they were afraid. ¹⁶ Those who had seen it told the people what had happened to the demon-possessed man—and told about the pigs as well. ¹⁷ Then the people began to plead with Jesus to leave their region.

¹⁸ As Jesus was getting into the boat, the man who had been demon-possessed begged to go with him. ¹⁹ Jesus did not let him, but said, "Go home to your own people and tell them how much the Lord has done

for you, and how he has had mercy on you." [20] So the man went away and began to tell in the Decapolis how much Jesus had done for him. And all the people were amazed.

Original Meaning

Wherever Jesus goes, his holy presence triggers a reaction from the unholy. The demons in this story do not cower in fear but cause the man to rush at Jesus. No one had the strength to "subdue" him. This Greek word (*damazō*) is used for taming a wild animal and is better translated, "no one was able to tame him." People treated him like a wild animal, and he acted like one. He was banished from society and had to dwell with those whose sleep would not be disturbed by his shrieks echoing through the night as he lacerated his body with stones.

In the demons' desperate attempt to resist being cast out, they are momentarily successful in creating a standoff. Their evasive tactics consist of having the demonized man prostrating himself before Jesus. Whether this action is counterfeit worship or conniving submission, the evil spirits employ subterfuge to persuade Jesus to leave them alone. They invoke the name of God to keep the Son of God off their back—to protect themselves.

Jesus asks for the demon's name. However, the evil spirits evade the question by giving a number instead of a name: "My name is Legion" (verse 9). A legion was the number in a Roman regiment consisting of six thousand foot soldiers and 120 horsemen. Mark reveals to his readers in this way that the man was captive to a *host* of demons.

It was popular belief in Mark's day that evil spirits were not content to wander aimlessly about. They wanted to inhabit *something*. A human host was best, but wanting that, a bunch of pigs would do. This is what the evil spirits request, and Jesus grants them passage. In this, he might seem too gracious in granting the request, but it leads to the surprise ending. The very thing the demons want to avert happens. From a

Jewish perspective, the scene is a joke. Unclean spirits and unclean animals are wiped out in one swoop, and a human is cleansed.

The townspeople do not seem to care that Jesus has such power. They just want him gone. Instead of giving him the key to the city, they give him a cold shoulder. The demons had begged Jesus to let them stay in the region, but the townspeople now beg Jesus to leave. But when Jesus is gone, a man transformed by the power of the Messiah remains as a witness!

❖ What did the demons acknowledge about Jesus and request of him? How did the townspeople acknowledge Jesus, and what request did they make of him?

_____

_____

_____

_____

_____

Past to Present

Look in the Mirror

We may see a mirror of ourselves in this disturbed man. He was beaten down by others, a civil war was raging within, and he lived among the gloomy tombs of life, feeling all alone. Yet if we can recognize ourselves in this tortured man, we can also recognize that deliverance is not just something that "other people" need. Deliverance is not reserved for just the "worst cases" like this man who was inhabited by thousands of demons.

Instead, the power of the gospel is also for *us*. We are just as battered as this man living among the tombs, though we may do a better job of hiding it behind our coherent words, our well-kept homes, and our sharp attire. What we need is the same thing this man needed. We need Jesus to land on the shore of our lives and quiet the forces of evil. Just as Jesus spoke to calm the wind and waves, and now calms this man, so he can bring calm into our lives.

❖ In what ways do you see yourself in the disturbed man in this story? How can you relate to what he might have been feeling as he lived among the tombs?

_____

_____

_____

_____

❖ What is an area of your life where you desire to be unchained (released from bondage)? What words do you need Jesus to speak over that situation today?

_____

_____

_____

_____

When Community Goes Wrong
Mark's original readers would have noticed the detail he goes into to describe how people in the man's community had tried to restrain him. They would also have noticed how members of this same community arrived on the scene after the deliverance to ask Jesus to leave. These details reveal that this story has to do not only with Jesus' encounter with the demons but also with that community—a community that cracks down on madmen and protects its own.

In fact, it is striking just how callously indifferent they are to the restoration of this man! They seem fine to have just left that man as he was, tortured and tearing himself up with stones in the graveyard. It is one thing to encounter the impersonal forces of evil in nature that run amok in an individual but quite another to encounter them in a *whole community*.

This provokes us to ponder our own motivations and responses when it comes to dealing with people like this man. Are we likewise content to just let them mire in their misery—that if they are out of our sight they are out of our minds? Or do we intentionally make a beeline for their shores like Jesus did? This community opted for violent solutions to problems. We, as followers of Jesus, must opt for solutions that encompass Jesus' way of compassion and mercy.

❖ How do you respond to the actions of the townspeople in this story? Why is it often easier to ignore those who are in pain rather than seek to help them?

_____

_____

_____

_____

_____

❖ What strongholds of fear are prevalent in your community? How does this story inspire you to stand against those strongholds?

_____

_____

_____

_____

_____

_____

Lord of Health and Lord over the Grave [Mark 5:21-43]

[21] When Jesus had again crossed over by boat to the other side of the lake, a large crowd gathered around him while he was by the lake. [22] Then one of the synagogue leaders, named Jairus, came, and when he saw Jesus, he fell at his feet. [23] He pleaded earnestly with him, "My little daughter is dying. Please come and put your hands on her so that she will be healed and live." [24] So Jesus went with him.

A large crowd followed and pressed around him. [25] And a woman was there who had been subject to bleeding for twelve years. [26] She had suffered a great deal under the care of many doctors and had spent all she had, yet instead of getting better she grew worse. [27] When she heard about Jesus, she came up behind him in the crowd and touched his cloak, [28] because she thought, "If I just touch his clothes, I will be healed." [29] Immediately her bleeding stopped and she felt in her body that she was freed from her suffering.

[30] At once Jesus realized that power had gone out from him. He turned around in the crowd and asked, "Who touched my clothes?"

[31] "You see the people crowding against you," his disciples answered, "and yet you can ask, 'Who touched me?'"

[32] But Jesus kept looking around to see who had done it. [33] Then the woman, knowing what had happened to her, came and fell at his feet and, trembling with fear, told him the whole truth. [34] He said to her, "Daughter, your faith has healed you. Go in peace and be freed from your suffering."

[35] While Jesus was still speaking, some people came from the house of Jairus, the synagogue leader. "Your daughter is dead," they said. "Why bother the teacher anymore?"

[36] Overhearing what they said, Jesus told him, "Don't be afraid; just believe."

[37] He did not let anyone follow him except Peter, James and John the brother of James. [38] When they came to the home of the synagogue leader, Jesus saw a commotion, with people crying and wailing loudly.

[39] He went in and said to them, "Why all this commotion and wailing? The child is not dead but asleep." [40] But they laughed at him.

After he put them all out, he took the child's father and mother and the disciples who were with him, and went in where the child was. [41] He took her by the hand and said to her, "*Talitha koum!*" (which means "Little girl, I say to you, get up!"). [42] Immediately the girl stood up and began to walk around (she was twelve years old). At this they were completely astonished. [43] He gave strict orders not to let anyone know about this, and told them to give her something to eat.

Original Meaning

Mark first presents Jesus' divine power over the natural world through the story of Jesus speaking to the storm and calming it. He then relates a story of Jesus speaking to a legion of demons and bringing calm to a man by casting out the demons into a herd of pigs. These stories reminded Mark's readers that Jesus, the one they served, was truly the Lord over nature and over the spiritual world. But there is one more set of stories that Mark wants to tell.

After Jesus returns from his journey across the lake, a synagogue official falls before his feet and begs him to come to his home and heal his daughter. Jesus agrees, but the rush to the girl's side is interrupted by an anonymous woman. She is so desperate to be healed from her illness that she sneaks up to touch Jesus' garments in hopes it will restore her to health.

This woman also suffers socially and psychologically. As a ritually "unclean" woman, she would have been ostracized from Jewish society. Her plight is further compounded because she has become impoverished by wasting her living on the fruitless cure of physicians. When she touches Jesus, immediately the flow of blood stops. Jesus calls her to step out in faith and be identified. When she does, he blesses her and announces that her faith has made her well.

One can only guess what the distraught father must be thinking about this delay. He, too, must then publicly demonstrate his trust in Jesus when the worst possible news comes. *His daughter is dead.* He had shown faith in coming to Jesus in the first place, and now he must continue when Jesus tells him not to fear. He leads Jesus to his house, where his faith is again challenged by the grievous chorus of those already assembled to mourn his little girl's death.

Their skepticism puts them outside. There will be no miracles for the scornful throng. In private—with only the parents and Peter, James, and John—Jesus grasps the little girl's hand and raises her up. Jesus does not utter some mysterious mumbo jumbo but an ordinary phrase. The offer of food shows that the child is really alive and not a disembodied spirit. The command to secrecy reveals that Jesus is not interested in turning jeers into cheers.

❖ How did both the synagogue leader and the woman show they had faith in Jesus?

_____

_____

_____

_____

_____

_____

Past to Present

Faith Has Many Faces

The miraculous healings in these two scenes reveal the power that comes through faith in Jesus. The synagogue official and the woman came to Jesus for healing because of their faith. They had faith in him *before* their healing—and that faith led to their being made well.

Whether it is halting or imperfect, faith compels us to reach for God when we need healing.

This occurs regardless of who is exhibiting the faith. The synagogue leader was in a different economic, social, and religious spectrum from the woman. He could openly approach Jesus with a direct request. The woman, however, had to slink around behind the scenes. This is why she felt she must approach Jesus from behind and merely try to touch his garments. What Mark reveals in this intertwined story is that being female, impure, dishonored, and destitute is no barrier to receiving help. In God's kingdom, the nobodies become somebody. This is important for us to remember. Regardless of what we think of ourselves, God sees us as his beloved children—and he is ready to help those who have faith.

❖ What do you learn from these stories about how God wants you to exercise your faith in him? When have you seen God move as a result of your faith?

❖ What are some barriers that people often set up when it comes to helping others? What does the story reveal about how God wants you to reach out and help others?

Faith Persists and Steps Forward

These two healings also reveal that faith shows persistence in the face of obstacles. The woman first had to overcome any shame she had in approaching Jesus and then overcome the large crowds that blocked her way to him. The synagogue official had to overcome the obstacle of the pronouncement of his daughter's death and believe that Jesus could still heal her. Both the woman and the synagogue leader had to overcome fear, push past barriers that threatened to sap their faith, and ultimately believe that Jesus would act on their behalf.

Faith is embodied in action. It is something that can be seen, like the synagogue leader approaching Jesus or the woman reaching out to touch his garment. It kneels, begs, and reaches out to touch. Faith does not wait to see if the waters will divide and then step out; it steps out first, trusting God to do what is needed. In our own lives, God will often call us to move out in faith before he releases his power in our lives. He wants us to trust him—and keep on praying and trusting him—as we seek him for help (see Luke 18:1).

❖ Where are some obstacles that God might be calling you to overcome when it comes to your faith? What is a specific obstacle that you sense he is calling you to bring to Jesus right now?

❖ Where do you most need strength from God to help you persevere in your faith? Who in your life could help you press forward in faith in this specific area of your life?

_____

_____

_____

_____

_____

_____

_____

_____

Closing Prayer: *Lord, help me walk in greater faith in you. When I face a storm, help me look to you and know you will calm the waves or ride with me through them. When the enemy attacks and demonic powers raise their voices, speak your words of deliverance and set me free. When my faith is ebbing and fear captures my heart, remind me that you heal, protect, deliver, and raise the dead. Lord of glory, be lord of my life this day and every day. Amen!*

The Ministry Expands

Mark 6:1-13, 30-44, 45-56

"Most likely to succeed" is a tagline often seen in high school yearbooks to denote that special student who is predicted to go far in life. When it comes to Jesus, it is safe to assume that no one voted him "most likely to succeed." His hometown of Nazareth was a small village, and no one expected a powerful spiritual leader to come from there. As one of his own disciples would proclaim, "Nazareth! Can anything good come from there?" (John 1:46).

Jesus grew up around siblings and friends. His family attended the local synagogue. He was a "carpenter" and likely had learned such skills from his father. For the casual observer, he might have seemed quite ordinary.

However, the people of Nazareth were now hearing reports of his expanding ministry. He had disciples. He was sending them out, in his name, with heavenly power to preach, cast out demons, and do miracles. Soon, they would hear accounts of Jesus walking on water and feeding the masses with a miraculous multiplication of bread and fish.

All this from the small-town boy who grew up right next door. As you might imagine, this created quite a buzz when Jesus returned to his hometown. There was a lot of speculation about who Jesus really was—and probably a bit of suspicion as well. After all, they had known him as just a local kid named Jesus. He was Joseph and Mary's son who grew up right in front of their eyes. They had not noticed anything "exceptional" about him.

The Ministry of the Apostles [Mark 6:1–13]

[1] Jesus left there and went to his hometown, accompanied by his disciples. [2] When the Sabbath came, he began to teach in the synagogue, and many who heard him were amazed.

"Where did this man get these things?" they asked. "What's this wisdom that has been given him? What are these remarkable miracles he is performing? [3] Isn't this the carpenter? Isn't this Mary's son and the brother of James, Joseph, Judas and Simon? Aren't his sisters here with us?" And they took offense at him.

[4] Jesus said to them, "A prophet is not without honor except in his own town, among his relatives and in his own home." [5] He could not do any miracles there, except lay his hands on a few sick people and heal them. [6] He was amazed at their lack of faith. Then Jesus went around teaching from village to village. [7] Calling the Twelve to him, he began to send them out two by two and gave them authority over impure spirits.

[8] These were his instructions: "Take nothing for the journey except a staff—no bread, no bag, no money in your belts. [9] Wear sandals but not an extra shirt. [10] Whenever you enter a house, stay there until you leave that town. [11] And if any place will not welcome you or listen to you, leave that place and shake the dust off your feet as a testimony against them."

[12] They went out and preached that people should repent. [13] They drove out many demons and anointed many sick people with oil and healed them.

Original Meaning

Mark gives his readers information about Jesus' background through the people's questions, "Isn't this the carpenter? Isn't this Mary's son?"

(verse 3). A "carpenter" (*tektōn*) could work with wood, metal, or stone, but in Jesus' context, it probably denoted a woodworking handyman. Jesus is identified as Mary's son, which is unusual, as normally a man was identified as the son of his father. This could perhaps be because his father was no longer alive and the people are expressing their familiarity with his mother. Regardless, the inference is that Jesus is simply "a local boy" who is one of them. They think they have Jesus pegged.

The upshot is that the Nazarenes are scandalized by him. This negative reaction makes their town little different from the region of the Gerasenes where the people asked Jesus to leave. Indeed, Mark reveals that Jesus could do no miracles there except heal a few people. So Jesus launches out and expands his mission by sending the twelve disciples to their unbelieving countrymen to preach repentance, cast out demons, and anoint the sick. He instructs them to accept the first accommodations offered. This demonstration of commitment is a testimony of their devotion to Jesus' mission and not to themselves.

Mark tells us nothing more about the results of their mission— whether it is successful or not. The best answer as to why is that Mark sees it as preparatory for the later mission of the disciples after Jesus' death and resurrection. It introduces them to the requirement of total self-sacrifice in their commitment and acquaints them with the reality of rejection. It therefore prepares them for Jesus' teaching about his destiny, which will follow.

❖ What do you think drove the people of Nazareth to resent Jesus? How did their lack of faith impact Jesus' ministry in their region?

Past to Present

Consider what this passage meant to the original readers and how it applies to us today.

The Problem with Familiarity

This story in Mark's Gospel reveals that when we judge others by appearances . . . we may be dead wrong. The people of Nazareth saw Jesus as a carpenter, not as the Messiah. He was blue collar just like them. In making this evaluation about Jesus based on outward appearances, they missed the truth about him—and likely misjudged his messengers.

Mark tells us the disciples accompanied Jesus to Nazareth, which would have provided them with great learning opportunities. The disciples saw the townspeople's indifferent response to Jesus' teaching and miracles, and they discovered that rejection will sometimes come when and where it is least expected. However, rejection is not the end of the world. Failure is common to the experience of anyone who sows the seeds of the gospel.

Another lesson to be gleaned from this passage is that familiarity can also breed contempt when it comes to our faith. There are many people today raised *in* the Christian faith who search for answers to life's questions by looking *outside* of their faith. Why is this the case? Perhaps because the stories about Jesus have become ordinary to them. Fascination with the unfamiliar and exotic can lead us to look for truth in what is new and different. We need to guard against this attitude about Jesus that was so prevalent among the people of Nazareth.

❖ Why is it easy to judge people based on first impressions? When is a time you made a judgment about someone that proved to be wrong?

❖ When have you encountered rejection when you were doing something you knew was in God's will? How did you respond to that situation?

_____

_____

_____

_____

_____

_____

_____

Lessons for the Journey of Faith

Mark provides us with several key principles about the disciple's mission that we can apply to the mission Jesus has given to each of us. First, the disciples' mission was an extension of Jesus' work in the world. They went as the "hands and feet" of Jesus to do his will in the world. Jesus will not do it all . . . he sends out *disciples* to help make ministry happen.

Second, the disciples were to be so dedicated to their mission that personal comforts were inconsequential. Jesus expected them to concentrate more on getting the message out than getting good accommodations. He did not promise a successful career or protection from sickness, ordeals, or tyrants. Likewise, we do not always get to choose where we will go. Answering the call to serve others is risky business, but ignoring it is even riskier.

Third, the disciples' mission involved not just preaching the good news but also bringing about the effects of the good news in people's lives through healing and deliverance. They offered people something that tangibly changed their lives. In the same way, Jesus calls us not only to proclaim the gospel but also to do the work of ministry and service that goes along with it. As James wrote, "Faith by itself, if it is not accompanied by action, is dead" (James 2:17).

❖ Why is it essential for Jesus' servants to be ready and willing to sacrifice in their service to him? How has God called you to do this in your life as a Christian?

_____

_____

_____

_____

_____

_____

❖ Why is it essential for Jesus' servants to be ready and willing to engage in acts of service? What is one specific way that you are responding to this call?

_____

_____

_____

_____

_____

_____

Jesus Feeds the Five Thousand [Mark 6:30-44]

30 The apostles gathered around Jesus and reported to him all they had done and taught. 31 Then, because so many people were coming and going that they did not even have a chance to eat, he said to them, "Come with me by yourselves to a quiet place and get some rest."

32 So they went away by themselves in a boat to a solitary place. 33 But many who saw them leaving recognized them and ran on foot from all the towns and got there ahead of them. 34 When Jesus landed and saw a large crowd, he had compassion on them, because they were like sheep without a shepherd. So he began teaching them many things.

³⁵ By this time it was late in the day, so his disciples came to him. "This is a remote place," they said, "and it's already very late. ³⁶ Send the people away so that they can go to the surrounding countryside and villages and buy themselves something to eat."

³⁷ But he answered, "You give them something to eat."

They said to him, "That would take more than half a year's wages! Are we to go and spend that much on bread and give it to them to eat?"

³⁸ "How many loaves do you have?" he asked. "Go and see."

When they found out, they said, "Five—and two fish."

³⁹ Then Jesus directed them to have all the people sit down in groups on the green grass. ⁴⁰ So they sat down in groups of hundreds and fifties. ⁴¹ Taking the five loaves and the two fish and looking up to heaven, he gave thanks and broke the loaves. Then he gave them to his disciples to distribute to the people. He also divided the two fish among them all. ⁴² They all ate and were satisfied, ⁴³ and the disciples picked up twelve basketfuls of broken pieces of bread and fish. ⁴⁴ The number of the men who had eaten was five thousand.

Original Meaning

A swarm of excited fans continue to besiege Jesus, making it impossible for him and his disciples to even take time to eat. This relentless pursuit of Jesus is further proof of his superstar popularity. Yet Jesus does not show any irritation with the crowds. Rather, he has compassion on them because they are "like a sheep without a shepherd" (verse 34).

Mark refrains from giving an account of Jesus' teaching, opting instead to tell about a miraculous feeding in the desert. When the disciples see it is getting late, they stress to Jesus they are in a deserted place and there is no way to feed the large crowd. Their outcry is reminiscent of Moses objecting when God told him to feed the Israelites (see Numbers 11:22) and Elisha's servant balking when asked to feed a company of prophets (see 2 Kings 4:43).

The story would have likely evoked several biblical themes in the original recipients' minds. First, it recalls God's miraculous provision of food in response to Moses' objection (see Numbers 11:31–32). Jesus likewise brings an abundance of food in spite of the disciples' objections. Second, the phrase "like sheep without a shepherd" (Mark 6:34) calls to mind the words of Psalm 23: "The Lord is my shepherd, I lack nothing" (verse 1). Jesus acts in his role as the "good shepherd" (John 10:11) to bring food and water to his sheep.

Third, the story from Mark calls to mind several stories that feature the prophets Elijah and Elisha. Elijah provided miraculously for the widow of Zarephath (see 1 Kings 17:8–16) and raised her son from the dead. Elisha fed the guild of a hundred prophets with twenty barley loaves (see 2 Kings 4:42–44). If we are meant to recall the works of these prophets of old, we see that in Jesus one greater than Elijah and Elisha has arrived in the world.

❖ What does this story reveal about the ways in which God provides for his people?

_____

_____

_____

_____

_____

Past to Present

The Role of the Shepherd

The image of Jesus as the good shepherd is prominent in this miracle of the feeding of the five thousand. To say the people were like sheep without a shepherd was a serious challenge to Israel's religious leadership. The problem was not that there were not enough priests to go around but that the religious leaders were not doing what they were meant to do. God had raised up these "shepherds of Israel" (Ezekiel 34:2) to guard, protect, and care for the sheep.

But when Jesus looked out, what he saw were spiritually and physically hungry people who were wrapped up in all sorts of religious red tape. In addition to being materially impoverished, they were also spiritually starved—and so he had compassion on them. When we look out in our world and see people in a similar state, our response should be the same as Jesus'. We step into the role of shepherd to seek out the lost, carry them back to the fold, and provide for them.

❖ What are some ways that God has called you to be a "shepherd" to his flock? How are you actively engaging in that role?

_____

_____

_____

_____

_____

❖ Would you say that you have the same reaction as Jesus when you see people in need? What needs to change in your perspective so you see people more like he did?

_____

_____

_____

_____

_____

Feed the Sheep

How many of us have voiced the same protests the disciples made? *The need is too great—there is nothing we can do that will matter. It will cost us too much to try and meet their need. Let them take care of themselves—they are not our responsibility.* As disciples of Jesus, we are called to do more than just lament the fact that there are hungry and needy people in our world. We are called to go into the world and do something about these problems.

In this story, the disciples were stymied when they thought the task was impossible for them or the cost was too great. It was only when they had the faith to trust the divine provision of God that they accomplished the job and provided everyone with enough. Jesus insisted that the disciples share in his ministry to the world and take responsibility for the crowd. He insists the same of us today—to feed the sheep and not just ourselves. Compassion combined with God's power can meet both the spiritual and physical needs of people.

❖ When is a time that you felt overwhelmed because you sensed a need was too great for you to fulfill? What did God reveal to you during that time?

_____

_____

_____

_____

_____

❖ In what ways do you sense Jesus is calling you to share in his ministry and take responsibility for those in your world who are in need?

_____

_____

_____

_____

_____

_____

Jesus Walks on the Water [Mark 6:45-56]

[45] Immediately Jesus made his disciples get into the boat and go on ahead of him to Bethsaida, while he dismissed the crowd. [46] After leaving them, he went up on a mountainside to pray.

[47] Later that night, the boat was in the middle of the lake, and he was alone on land. [48] He saw the disciples straining at the oars, because the wind was against them. Shortly before dawn he went out to them, walking on the lake. He was about to pass by them, [49] but when they saw him walking on the lake, they thought he was a ghost. They cried out, [50] because they all saw him and were terrified.

Immediately he spoke to them and said, "Take courage! It is I. Don't be afraid." [51] Then he climbed into the boat with them, and the wind died down. They were completely amazed, [52] for they had not understood about the loaves; their hearts were hardened.

[53] When they had crossed over, they landed at Gennesaret and anchored there. [54] As soon as they got out of the boat, people recognized Jesus. [55] They ran throughout that whole region and carried the sick on mats to wherever they heard he was. [56] And wherever he went—into villages, towns or countryside—they placed the sick in the marketplaces. They begged him to let them touch even the edge of his cloak, and all who touched it were healed.

Original Meaning

The miracle of the feeding of the five thousand is followed by another ordeal at sea. This time, the storm does not endanger the disciples' lives. Rather, they are stuck in the middle of the lake, fighting against the wind after hours of strenuous rowing. Jesus does not immediately rescue them but uses the situation to teach them a lesson. He walks by them, striding on the surface of the waves, but their eyes and ears are not up to it. They see only a ghost—and panic.

Jesus displays his divine power when he gets into the boat and the winds cease to howl. Yet this does not calm the disciples' apprehension. Mark offers a surprising explanation for their amazement: "They had not understood about the loaves; their hearts were hardened" (verse 52). Clearly, the two incidents are connected. What is it that the disciples do not understand about the loaves? What does it have to do with Jesus walking on the water?

The disciples are blind to the presence of God in their midst and his care for them. They have missed the significance of the miracle of the loaves just witnessed and now only see a marvel. They are also hard-hearted, which refers to being disobedient, dull, and obstinate—much the way in which Jesus' opponents are described (see Mark 3:5). Yet there is a difference. The disciples may be confused and blind, but they are not hostile to Jesus.

Jesus never gives up on the disciples in spite of their failures. Rather, he takes them through the whole process again once they reach the other side so they can gain more understanding. Jesus does not require them to grasp things immediately . . . for *complete* understanding will not come to them until after his death and resurrection.

❖ Why do you think the disciples failed to recognize it was Jesus walking to them? How did Jesus calm their fears and reveal it was him?

Past to Present

Rowing Against the Storm

Mark's story about another storm on the Sea of Galilee provides us with an important principle about rest. Jesus had previously called the disciples to come away with him to a quiet place to get some rest (see Mark 6:31). After the miracle of the feeding of the five thousand, he retreated to spend some time in prayer (see verse 46). We all need solitude, rest, and prayer—and it is in such moments we can hear God speak most clearly.

Meanwhile, the disciples were separated from Jesus. They had been instructed to go to the other side, but they were getting nowhere despite all their rowing. Many of us feel the same way when we serve! We keep rowing so we can move forward in our mission but seem to make no progress. Discouragement sets in when we feel we are headed into a gale. It is in such times that we need to follow Jesus' example to retreat and refocus on God.

It is significant that Jesus does not rescue his disciples from the storm but enables them to continue the voyage. Even though they cannot see Jesus, he can see them, and he comes to them in their hour of need. Jesus knows what they are going through on the sea. When he climbs into the boat, they suddenly have the ability to reach the other side—though they must keep on rowing. In the same way, God will give us the ability to reach the "other side" of whatever we are facing. But we must trust in his presence and keep on rowing.

❖ Why is it so important to engage in solitude, rest, and prayer? How have you seen the benefits of these three things in your life?

_____

_____

_____

_____

_____

❖ When is a time that Jesus revealed he was with you in the storm? How did Jesus enable you to keep rowing and reach the "other side"?

_____

_____

_____

_____

_____

_____

_____

_____

Closing Prayer: *Jesus, help me never grow so familiar with your presence in my life that I become apathetic. Teach me new truths that enliven my spirit and engage my mind. Let my life be an adventure of faith that grows stronger and stronger so I can follow you and pursue your mission all the days of my life. For your glory, amen.*

The One Who Cleanses

Mark 7:1–15, 24–30, 31–37

In our world today, we don't ask who is "clean" or "unclean" in the church. But we do have spoken and unspoken tendencies toward judgment, boundary keeping, and even disgust with others. In short, we still decide who is *in* and who is *out*. In Mark's Gospel, we see that Jesus has a tendency to unsettle people who make such distinctions. He challenges them to put their faith in him instead of human religious standards. Ultimately, he challenges all of his disciples to examine their own need for cleansing instead of pointing at others.

Who needs cleansing? It depends on who you ask. The religious leaders of Jesus' day were sure they were clean—and they had a good idea of who was not quite as good as them. These Pharisees and teachers of the law were quick to point out who was falling short of the religious standards of the time. Yet when Jesus came along, he made it crystal clear that even these pious and devout leaders were in desperate need of cleansing.

In fact, as Mark reveals in this next section of his Gospel, everyone needed the touch of Jesus to make them clean and pure in the sight of God. Jews and Gentiles. Men and women. Insiders and outsiders. This extends to us today. We all need the touch of Jesus. The good news is that Jesus is delighted to give that touch lavishly to all who ask.

What Defiles and What Cleanses? [Mark 7:1-15]

[1] The Pharisees and some of the teachers of the law who had come from Jerusalem gathered around Jesus [2] and saw some of his disciples eating food with hands that were defiled, that is, unwashed. [3] (The Pharisees and all the Jews do not eat unless they give their hands a ceremonial washing, holding to the tradition of the elders. [4] When they come from the marketplace they do not eat unless they wash. And they observe many other traditions, such as the washing of cups, pitchers and kettles.)

[5] So the Pharisees and teachers of the law asked Jesus, "Why don't your disciples live according to the tradition of the elders instead of eating their food with defiled hands?"

[6] He replied, "Isaiah was right when he prophesied about you hypocrites; as it is written:

"'These people honor me with their lips,
    but their hearts are far from me.
[7] They worship me in vain;
    their teachings are merely human rules.'

[8] You have let go of the commands of God and are holding on to human traditions."

[9] And he continued, "You have a fine way of setting aside the commands of God in order to observe your own traditions! [10] For Moses said, 'Honor your father and mother,' and, 'Anyone who curses their father or mother is to be put to death.' [11] But you say that if anyone declares that what might have been used to help their father or mother is Corban (that is, devoted to God)— [12] then you no longer let them do anything for their father or mother. [13] Thus you nullify the word of God by your tradition that you have handed down. And you do many things like that."

[14] Again Jesus called the crowd to him and said, "Listen to me, everyone, and understand this. [15] Nothing outside a person can defile them by going into them. Rather, it is what comes out of a person that defiles them."

Original Meaning

The conflict in this story revolves around the issue of defilement. The Pharisees accuse the disciples of eating with hands that are "defiled" or "unwashed." The Levitical system regarded uncleanness as something that was transferable to people, vessels, clothes, and even houses through touch, lying, or sitting. When Mark says "the Pharisees and all the Jews" perform this ceremonial washing, it implies that to be Jewish, a person followed this practice.

Jesus cites an extreme example in his counterattack to show how the tradition of the Pharisees sanctions the subversion of God's will. He states that God commands children to honor their parents, which in Jewish tradition requires them to provide their parents with physical necessities. However, under the Pharisees' way of thinking, a son could shirk that responsibility by telling his parents that the support they expected to get from him is "Corban"—that is, dedicated to God—and therefore it cannot be touched to help them.

From Jesus' point of view, the command to honor one's parents soars above the command to honor vows. Therefore, any such *vow* in this case is automatically invalid because it violates God's *command* to honor parents. A person cannot elude God's commands by resorting to legal loopholes! Jesus thus exposes these sticklers for the law as being more interested in legal niceties than the requirement of love, more devoted to unwritten traditions than the written law, and more concerned with property than care of one's parents.

❖ How do the Pharisees and teachers of the law define *defilement* in this passage? What does Jesus say is the bigger issue at stake here?

Past to Present

Consider what this passage meant to the original readers and how it applies to us today.

Bridges . . . Not Fences

Many people engage in heated religious arguments over what they regard to be life-and-death issues that, to the outside world, are a lot of fuss about nothing. This is what the Pharisees were doing by defining what was proper and pure (which represented their sacred tradition) and what was improper and impure. It is something we do in our own religious traditions.

The problem is that such definitions can be used to turn the Christian faith into an unassailable fortress that keeps the pure *in* and the impure *out*. Those who are defined as impure remain on the outside, while those classified as pure stay on the inside. Such a system, of course, closes the door to those on the outside who know they are impure but very much want to come inside and learn how to be pure. Rather than inviting those who are far from God into fellowship with him, it keeps the lost left out in the dark.

This is clearly not the desire of Jesus, who said, "The Son of Man came to seek and to save the lost" (Luke 19:10). It is also something the apostle Paul warned Christians against doing when he told one group of believers, "Therefore let us stop passing judgment on one another. Instead, make up your mind not to put any stumbling block or obstacle in the way of a brother or sister" (Romans 14:13). This forces us to ask ourselves, *Are there subtle and not so subtle ways we are communicating to others that they are "dirty" and unfit to come into our church?*

Of course, this doesn't mean that no boundaries are drawn at all. Jesus followed God's laws, and so should we. He also continually confounded with how he could welcome unexpected people into his presence. As his followers, we should be known for the same attitude.

❖ How have you seen people in the church engage in religious debates that are "a lot of fuss about nothing"? When have *you* engaged in these kinds of debates?

_____

_____

_____

_____

_____

_____

❖ What do you do to break down any religious traditions or barriers that might discourage those who are on the "outside" from coming into a relationship with Jesus?

_____

_____

_____

_____

_____

The Faith of an Outsider [Mark 7:24-30]

24 Jesus left that place and went to the vicinity of Tyre. He entered a house and did not want anyone to know it; yet he could not keep his presence secret. 25 In fact, as soon as she heard about him, a woman whose little daughter was possessed by an impure spirit came and fell at his feet. 26 The woman was a Greek, born in Syrian Phoenicia. She begged Jesus to drive the demon out of her daughter.

27 "First let the children eat all they want," he told her, "for it is not right to take the children's bread and toss it to the dogs."

²⁸ "Lord," she replied, "even the dogs under the table eat the children's crumbs."

²⁹ Then he told her, "For such a reply, you may go; the demon has left your daughter."

³⁰ She went home and found her child lying on the bed, and the demon gone.

Original Meaning

Jesus' next destination is the region of Tyre. When word leaks out that he is in the vicinity, a woman whose daughter is a victim of an unclean spirit immediately begins to hunt for him to ask for his help. We see a token of her faith in seeking him out and her resourceful determination when she detects his whereabouts. She is a Gentile pagan, which introduces a wrinkle in the story. Gentiles were considered impure simply because they were Gentiles. The humble request of this gentile woman, therefore, creates dramatic tension for Mark's readers. Will Jesus be as gracious to her as he was to the unclean outcasts within Israel?

The resulting exchange comes with many surprises. Jesus first dismisses her appeal out of hand with a sharp insult. The word *first* (verse 27) implies that Gentiles have some ray of hope, but for the time being, this woman must wait for her turn. Jesus comes as the Messiah of *Israel*, and she has no right to jump the queue to receive benefits from him.

However, the woman is unwilling to be put off by this less-than-genial response. She recognizes, without any prompting, that "children" in the parable Jesus has just stated represent Israel and "dogs" represent Gentiles. She accepts the riddle's implications: Israel has precedence over Gentiles, and the time for the Gentiles has not yet come.

The implied insult does not embitter her. Instead, she becomes the first person in Mark's Gospel to engage Jesus in a constructive exchange about his mission. She does not deny Israel's preeminence—yet, at the same time, she refuses to take no for an answer. She is not asking for a full-course meal, just a crumb of Jesus' power. What is Jesus' response to her doggedness? "For such a reply, you may go; the demon has left your daughter" (verse 29).

❖ How do you react to how Jesus initially responds to the woman? What was he saying to her through the sharp comment he made?

_____

_____

_____

_____

_____

Past to Present

Humility to the Lord

The woman's response reveals that she comprehends more about the "bread" that Jesus offers than his disciples do. This woman—who did not partake in the feeding of the five thousand as the disciples did—begs to receive only the bread crumbs falling from the diners' laps. She knows she cannot insist on God's mercy and does not take offense when Jesus tells her so. She will gladly accept the rank of household dog if it means getting fed.

The woman's witty comeback to Jesus expresses sincere humility. She concedes the differences between children (the Jews) and dogs (the Gentiles). She accepts Jewish priority—the bread rightly belongs first to Israel. The woman's willingness to humble herself is a requirement for all who seek to be disciples of Jesus. As James wrote, "Humble yourselves before the Lord, and he will lift you up" (James 4:10). We cannot presume to make demands on God. However, when we come humbly before him, as the woman in this story did, we find that he responds to our humility and lifts us up.

❖ How do you typically respond when you receive what seems like an insult from others?

_____

_____

_____

_____

❖ In what ways is it difficult for you to show humility like the woman did in this story?

_____

_____

_____

_____

Trusting Faith in Jesus

When Jesus tells the Syrophoenician woman the demon has left her daughter, she does not insist that he go back with her to make sure. We see her leave in faith just as she had come in faith. She stands in contrast to the Pharisees who rebuked Jesus' disciples for eating with unwashed hands. They had implied the disciples were too unclean to eat at their table. But this Gentile woman—who was at the bottom rung of the ladder when it came to being clean or unclean—was willing to approach Jesus in faith and take the breadcrumbs. The group of Pharisees received a rebuke from Jesus. The woman received the healing of her daughter. It matters how we approach God. The Lord wants us to come to him not only in humility but also with a heart of faith.

❖ What tends to get in the way the most when it comes to approaching Jesus in faith?

_____

_____

_____

❖ How does this story encourage you that no one is too "unclean" to approach God?

_____

_____

_____

_____

_____

_____

The Power of Persistence

There is one other notable trait that we find in the Syrophoenician woman. She not only approached Jesus in faith, and responded to him in humility, but she also demonstrated persistence. The woman in this story was no doormat. She aggressively sought help from Jesus and would not be turned away. She knew she was unworthy, but that didn't keep her from believing that she and her daughter were *worth* healing. The woman was like a man in one of Jesus' parables who kept on knocking on his friend's door at midnight asking for bread. Jesus said, "Even though he will not get up and give you the bread because of friendship, yet because of your shameless audacity he will surely get up and give you as much as you need" (Luke 11:8). God rewards those who are faithful in coming to him—again and again and again—in prayer.

❖ Why do you think God instructs you to be persistent in your requests to him?

_____

_____

_____

_____

_____

❖ What are some ways you demonstrate persistence in your prayers? What results have you witnessed as a result of your persistence?

_____

_____

_____

Jesus Heals a Deaf and Mute Man [Mark 7:31-37]

[31] Then Jesus left the vicinity of Tyre and went through Sidon, down to the Sea of Galilee and into the region of the Decapolis. [32] There some people brought to him a man who was deaf and could hardly talk, and they begged Jesus to place his hand on him.

[33] After he took him aside, away from the crowd, Jesus put his fingers into the man's ears. Then he spit and touched the man's tongue. [34] He looked up to heaven and with a deep sigh said to him, "*Ephphatha!*" (which means "Be opened!"). [35] At this, the man's ears were opened, his tongue was loosened and he began to speak plainly.

[36] Jesus commanded them not to tell anyone. But the more he did so, the more they kept talking about it. [37] People were overwhelmed with amazement. "He has done everything well," they said. "He even makes the deaf hear and the mute speak."

Original Meaning

Mark has already related several stories about healings that Jesus performed. But the location of this particular healing is noteworthy. The mention of Tyre, Sidon, and the Decapolis emphasizes that Jesus is in *Gentile* territory. Just as the Jewish crowds brought their sick to Jesus, so now a Gentile crowd brings a deaf and speechless man to him.

Jesus uses a sequence of actions in this healing rather than just a spoken word. In many ways, these actions are symbolic. Jesus puts his fingers in the man's ears, symbolic of opening them. He spits and touches the man's tongue, symbolic of loosening his tongue. Then he looks up to heaven, the source of his power, and sighs deeply—a symbol of prayer. Finally, Jesus says "*Ephphatha*," an Aramaic word that simply means, "Be opened!" (verse 34).

Jesus can command storms, demons, and illnesses, but the orders he gives the people to keep silent about this miracle fall on deaf ears. They jabber about what Jesus has done, though the magnitude of what it signifies escapes them. Nevertheless, they proclaim the *truth* even though they do not fully understand it, saying, "He has done everything well" (verse 37).

❖ What was unique about this healing? Why do you think Jesus healed the man in stages?

Past to Present

Hearing God's Voice

When Jesus finished telling the parable of the sower, he said to the crowd, "Whoever has ears to hear, let them hear" (Mark 4:9). The problem is that many of the people of God—like the self-righteous Pharisees—suffered from an acute form of spiritual deafness. Meanwhile, Mark shows that at least one person among the Gentiles—the Syrophoenician woman—showed great openness to hearing what Jesus had to say.

We learn a similar lesson from the physically deaf man brought before Jesus in the Decapolis. Jesus healed him, but he also desired to heal his people's spiritual deafness. Sadly, spiritual deafness is still prevalent among God's people today. Perhaps we are deafened to God's voice by the ceaseless distractions that are all too present in our world today. Perhaps we fail to hear God's voice clearly because the hurry and stress of modern life has drowned it out.

Mark reveals that Jesus sought to cure his disciples' spiritual deafness (and blindness) by taking them away from the crowds regularly and teaching them directly. Likewise, there are times when we may need to retreat from the world so we can hear God's voice. We need to find a place away from all the distractions so the miracle of Jesus' power can penetrate our plugged-up ears. In this way, we can hear God's words anew and speak it to others more clearly.

❖ What are some of the things that keep you from hearing the words of God? What can you do to find quiet places where you can listen and learn from the Lord?

_____

_____

_____

_____

❖ Think about a time you were able to slow down, quiet down, and tune in to God. How did God speak, move, and give you direction when you did this?

_____

_____

_____

_____

Closing Prayer: *God of the religious elite and the wandering pagan, you meet us right where we are. You come with firm truth and piercing clarity as you speak to your children. Meet us where we are today. Wake us up and shake us with your Word and truth. We are ready to hear, we want to be transformed, and we long to hear your voice. Amen.*

7

Missing the Point

Mark 8:1-21; 27-38; 9:2-15

You respond to a statement your friend has just made with what you believe is a thoughtful comment. But the confusion you see in her eyes reveals that something is amiss. Suddenly, it dawns on your friend what has happened. She chuckles and says, "Oh, no, that's not what I meant." You have *missed the point* of what was being said.

This happens to us all the time. So it should be comforting to know that even Jesus' disciples missed the point of what he was saying and doing at times. The crowds who came to Jesus also missed the point again and again. They seemed to want physical bread more than the "true bread from heaven" that Jesus offered (John 6:32). Even the Jewish religious leaders, with all their knowledge of the Scriptures and supposed wisdom, had no idea what God was doing right in front of their eyes. Everyone seemed to miss the point when it came to Jesus!

It's likely that if we had walked in the sandals of these ancient people, we would have also missed the point of what Jesus was saying, doing, and teaching. Many people today—even with the advantage of having the New Testament and Gospels like Mark—miss the point. However, if we are willing, Jesus can help us to understand. He will illuminate the truth so it guides our way and helps us build a faith that has a strong foundation.

Feeding of the Four Thousand [Mark 8:1–21]

[1] During those days another large crowd gathered. Since they had nothing to eat, Jesus called his disciples to him and said, [2] "I have compassion for these people; they have already been with me three days and have nothing to eat. [3] If I send them home hungry, they will collapse on the way, because some of them have come a long distance."

[4] His disciples answered, "But where in this remote place can anyone get enough bread to feed them?"

[5] "How many loaves do you have?" Jesus asked.

"Seven," they replied.

[6] He told the crowd to sit down on the ground. When he had taken the seven loaves and given thanks, he broke them and gave them to his disciples to distribute to the people, and they did so. [7] They had a few small fish as well; he gave thanks for them also and told the disciples to distribute them. [8] The people ate and were satisfied. Afterward the disciples picked up seven basketfuls of broken pieces that were left over. [9] About four thousand were present. After he had sent them away, [10] he got into the boat with his disciples and went to the region of Dalmanutha.

[11] The Pharisees came and began to question Jesus. To test him, they asked him for a sign from heaven. [12] He sighed deeply and said, "Why does this generation ask for a sign? Truly I tell you, no sign will be given to it."

[13] Then he left them, got back into the boat and crossed to the other side.

[14] The disciples had forgotten to bring bread, except for one loaf they had with them in the boat. [15] "Be careful," Jesus warned them. "Watch out for the yeast of the Pharisees and that of Herod."

[16] They discussed this with one another and said, "It is because we have no bread."

[17] Aware of their discussion, Jesus asked them: "Why are you talking about having no bread? Do you still not see or understand? Are your

hearts hardened? [18] Do you have eyes but fail to see, and ears but fail to hear? And don't you remember? [19] When I broke the five loaves for the five thousand, how many basketfuls of pieces did you pick up?"

"Twelve," they replied.

[20] "And when I broke the seven loaves for the four thousand, how many basketfuls of pieces did you pick up?"

They answered, "Seven."

[21] He said to them, "Do you still not understand?"

Original Meaning

The feeding of the four thousand occurs while Jesus is still in "the region of the Decapolis" (Mark 7:31). This context suggests that Jesus is now offering a predominantly Gentile crowd the same opportunity to be fed by his teaching and power that he offered to the Jewish crowd. Mark's readers would have seen in this that Jesus came to be the redeemer of the *entire* world.

The account highlights the lack of growth taking place in the disciples, for they ask a similar question of Jesus as they did in the feeding of the five thousand: "Where in this remote place can anyone get enough bread to feed them?" (verse 4). Jesus, like before, has them go through their provisions—this time, they have seven loaves. The disciples still do not realize that even with such scanty supplies, they have in Jesus enough to feed the entire world.

Jesus moves on to Dalmanutha, where he is met by a group of Pharisees who ask for "a sign from heaven" (verse 11). Jesus recognizes these Pharisees are asking for him to provide a sign that will conform to their goals and aspirations before they will commit to believing in him—and so he refuses to provide one. Later, back in the boat, Jesus warns his disciples not to fall victim to this same unbelief. The disciples, however, have only brought one loaf of bread with them and are worried about where their next meal will come from. This makes them deaf to Jesus' warning about not hearing and blind to the warning against spiritual blindness!

Jesus states that the feedings in the desert should explain everything to them. The signs the disciples have witnessed should point them toward recognizing that he is the Messiah who works according to the power of God. Yet, sadly, the disciples remain mired in their own little world with its petty alarms and cannot see God's reign breaking into their midst.

❖ What are some of the differences between the feeding of the four thousand and the feeding of the five thousand? What aspects of the story are similar?

_____

_____

_____

_____

_____

_____

Past to Present

Consider what this passage meant to the original readers and how it applies to us today.

Jesus Sees the Need

Mark's original readers—like us—would have been prompted to compare this second feeding miracle to the first. A close reading reveals that both miracles occur in a desert place, both come about as a result of Jesus' compassion for the crowd, and both feature an exchange between Jesus and his disciples. A significant difference, however, is where the miracles occur. Unlike the feeding of the five thousand, this miracle takes place in a Gentile region.

In the first miracle, Jesus says the crowd is like "sheep without a shepherd" (Mark 6:34)—a description frequently used in the Old Testament to describe the plight of the Israelites (see 1 Kings 22:17; Ezekiel 34:5). In that miracle, it is the *disciples* who raise the concern about the needs of the (predominantly Jewish) crowd. However, in the second miracle, we read that Jesus simply has "compassion for these people" (Mark 8:2) and that it is *he* who raises the concern about the hunger of this (predominantly Gentile) crowd.

If Mark intends us to see ourselves represented in this feeding, we can take comfort in the fact that Jesus recognizes our need. The promises that we read about concerning God's kingdom include each of us. All people are welcome into the family of God.

❖ When is a time that Jesus reached out and met a specific need for you? How did he accomplish this—and how did you know he was the one meeting the need?

_____

_____

_____

_____

_____

❖ We are more like the disciples than we wish to admit. Why do you think it is often so hard to look outside of our own "groups" when it comes to helping others?

_____

_____

_____

_____

_____

_____

Jesus Is Patient

One point that remains consistent in each of the feeding miracles is the reaction of the disciples. Each time, they ask Jesus how they can possibly secure enough food to feed the crowd. They have quickly forgotten how Jesus just provided a bounteous meal in a similar situation. The disciples do not come across well in this regard—yet that does not mean they are opponents of Jesus. They simply do not yet fully see or understand what Jesus came to do on this earth. They remain in the dark about what the kingdom of God looks like.

The narrative that Mark relates does its work when we can see our own spiritual blindness in the disciples' blindness. They were seeing and hearing Jesus through the lens of their traditional view of the world—a view warped by their dreams, ambitions, and immediate needs. The way we look at the world is no different . . . and we are in no less need of Jesus' patience in guiding us to see things as he sees them. Fortunately, Jesus' interactions with the disciples reveal that he never gave up on them. Likewise, he will not give up on us.

❖ How does remembering what Jesus has done for you in the past help you to trust in his provision for the future?

_____

_____

_____

_____

❖ What are some things in your life that might be blinding you to the work that Jesus is doing in your midst?

_____

_____

_____

_____

Peter's Declaration [Mark 8:27–38]

[27] Jesus and his disciples went on to the villages around Caesarea Philippi. On the way he asked them, "Who do people say I am?"

[28] They replied, "Some say John the Baptist; others say Elijah; and still others, one of the prophets."

[29] "But what about you?" he asked. "Who do you say I am?"

Peter answered, "You are the Messiah."

[30] Jesus warned them not to tell anyone about him.

[31] He then began to teach them that the Son of Man must suffer many things and be rejected by the elders, the chief priests and the teachers of the law, and that he must be killed and after three days rise again. [32] He spoke plainly about this, and Peter took him aside and began to rebuke him.

[33] But when Jesus turned and looked at his disciples, he rebuked Peter. "Get behind me, Satan!" he said. "You do not have in mind the concerns of God, but merely human concerns."

[34] Then he called the crowd to him along with his disciples and said: "Whoever wants to be my disciple must deny themselves and take up their cross and follow me. [35] For whoever wants to save their life will lose it, but whoever loses their life for me and for the gospel will save it. [36] What good is it for someone to gain the whole world, yet forfeit their soul? [37] Or what can anyone give in exchange for their soul? [38] If anyone is ashamed of me and my words in this adulterous and sinful generation, the Son of Man will be ashamed of them when he comes in his Father's glory with the holy angels."

Original Meaning

Jesus' questions to his disciples in this section of Mark's Gospel are intended to get at the heart of what *they* believe about him. So far, the disciples have only called him "Teacher" (4:38), though they have asked themselves the question, "Who is this?" (4:41). Peter responds to Jesus' question by proclaiming, "You are the Messiah" (8:29). This confession represents a significant leap of faith on his part, as Jewish expectations of the Messiah were that he would be a great political leader. Peter appears to be seeing clearly with spiritual eyes.

However, when Jesus goes on to explain it is necessary for the Son of Man to suffer and die, Peter and the rest of the disciples are plunged back into an uncomprehending daze. They cannot grasp that Jesus' suffering, rejection, and death as the Messiah are all part of God's plan and have to do with his hidden way of salvation. So Peter steps up and tries to set Jesus straight. He calls Jesus aside and "rebukes" him for being so mistaken as to think that the Messiah will ever have to suffer. Peter has begun to understand that Jesus' great manifestation of power means that he must be the Messiah, but he does not have any understanding of how Jesus' crucifixion, death, and resurrection tie into his identity.

Peter thus shows himself at cross-purposes with Jesus. He wants to impose his own private agenda on how Jesus will live out his vocation as Messiah and how he and the rest of the disciples will benefit as his followers. Jesus heals this spiritual blindness in Peter with a rebuke—he turns around, looks at the disciples, and calls Peter "Satan." Peter, without realizing it, has set himself against the plan of God and thus lined himself up behind Satan. Being a disciple of Jesus means more than just getting his title right. True disciples, Jesus goes on to explain, also deny themselves, take up a cross, and follow the way he has chosen.

❖ In what ways is Peter getting some of the picture of who Jesus is? In what ways is he still missing the point of who the Messiah is and what he came to do?

Past to Present

Dealing with Rebuke

Mark's readers would have seen in this story that Jesus not only had to contend with the false expectations of his rivals but also with the wishful fantasies of his supporters. For the moment, the religious leaders of Israel were a lost cause, so Jesus concentrated his energies on helping the disciples unlearn everything they had been taught about the role of the Messiah. They had to learn that victory would come through the *giving* of a life, not by *taking* others' lives.

We should be aware of how much we, like Peter, tend to project our aspirations on Jesus. The truth is that we also like to correct Jesus' teaching at times to suit our own worldview, particularly when it comes to the theme of suffering and sacrifice. But when we do this, we can expect to receive a "rebuke" from Jesus. However, just as Jesus' rebuke of Peter was not a sign of rejection, so any rebuke we receive from God will not be a sign of his rejection of us. Rather, God uses such rebukes to challenge us and get us back in line with his way of thinking. God wants us to have an accurate understanding about the role of his Son.

❖ What are some of the faulty assumptions you have held about God in the past? How did God help you to "unlearn" those faulty views?

❖ How do you know when God is challenging you to get back in line with his way of thinking? How do you typically respond when he does this in your life?

_____

_____

_____

_____

_____

_____

The Cost of Being a Disciple

Thankfully, Jesus did not just rebuke Peter, call him "Satan," and walk away. Instead, he went on to acquaint the disciples (and others who wanted to follow after him) with the rigors that are required of being a true disciple of the Messiah. Jesus first states that those who want to follow after him must *deny themselves*. Those who do this learn to say, "Not my will, God, but yours be done." True disciples get rid of *anything* that hinders them from giving their lives over to God.

Second, Jesus demands that his disciples *take up a cross*. This imagery would have sounded strange to Jesus' listeners at the time, but it nevertheless communicated danger and sacrifice. It is not enough for us to merely confess that Jesus is the Messiah. If he is the Messiah, then he expects to be followed and obeyed. Jesus does not ask for modest adjustments in our lives but a complete overhaul of our behavior.

Third, Jesus tells us to *follow the way he has chosen*. The wisdom of this world will always tell us that Jesus' ways are counterintuitive to how we should lead our lives. Jesus' message of serving others and loving them clashes with the world's message of continually looking out for ourselves and loving others only when it benefits us. Jesus turns conventional wisdom on its head, yet it is a requirement of all true disciples to follow what he says.

❖ True disciples get rid of anything that hinders them from giving their lives over to God. What are some things Jesus has called you to leave behind in order to follow after him?

_____

_____

_____

_____

❖ What are some of the things the world has whispered to you as you have sought to follow Christ? How have you been able to disregard those voices?

_____

_____

_____

_____

The Transfiguration [Mark 9:2–15]

2 After six days Jesus took Peter, James and John with him and led them up a high mountain, where they were all alone. There he was transfigured before them. 3 His clothes became dazzling white, whiter than anyone in the world could bleach them. 4 And there appeared before them Elijah and Moses, who were talking with Jesus.

5 Peter said to Jesus, "Rabbi, it is good for us to be here. Let us put up three shelters—one for you, one for Moses and one for Elijah." 6 (He did not know what to say, they were so frightened.)

7 Then a cloud appeared and covered them, and a voice came from the cloud: "This is my Son, whom I love. Listen to him!"

8 Suddenly, when they looked around, they no longer saw anyone with them except Jesus.

⁹ As they were coming down the mountain, Jesus gave them orders not to tell anyone what they had seen until the Son of Man had risen from the dead. ¹⁰ They kept the matter to themselves, discussing what "rising from the dead" meant.

¹¹ And they asked him, "Why do the teachers of the law say that Elijah must come first?"

¹² Jesus replied, "To be sure, Elijah does come first, and restores all things. Why then is it written that the Son of Man must suffer much and be rejected? ¹³ But I tell you, Elijah has come, and they have done to him everything they wished, just as it is written about him."

¹⁴ When they came to the other disciples, they saw a large crowd around them and the teachers of the law arguing with them. ¹⁵ As soon as all the people saw Jesus, they were overwhelmed with wonder and ran to greet him.

Original Meaning

The action now moves forward six days in time. Jesus takes Peter, James, and John up a high mountain. There, Jesus is "transfigured" before them, and his clothes become dazzlingly white. A voice speaks from a cloud, and later the people are astonished when they see Jesus. Mark's Jewish readers would have seen the connection between this account and Moses' meeting with God on Mount Sinai. Moses, like Jesus, went with three named persons up the mountain (see Exodus 24:9), his skin shone after the encounter (see verse 29), a voice spoke to him from a cloud (see verse 16), and the people were astonished when they saw him (see verse 30).

The mention of Moses' and Elijah's presence is significant, as it speaks to the Jewish hopes about the final redemption of Israel and suggests the time has been fulfilled. Yet once again, we find the disciples missing the point. Peter's response to what he sees makes it clear that he still does not comprehend what is happening. He continues to see and react to things from a human perspective—and fear continues to cloud his mind. If his offer to build three shelters suggests a desire on his part to venerate the three figures, he has failed to recognize Jesus' rank. Elijah and Moses, great as they were, do not share God's glory with Jesus.

The disciples' question about Elijah appearing before the coming of the great Day of the Lord—which would launch an earthly kingdom of messianic splendor—shows they were still listening to the teachers of the law. If Elijah came before the Day of the Lord, when the Messiah was to be in his earthly kingdom, then how could the Messiah be dead and need to be resurrected? Jesus responds by informing them Elijah has *already come*. Clearly, he has John the Baptist in mind, who came to announce the coming of the Messiah. "Elijah's" return would thus not herald the approach of messianic happy days. The disciples had to rethink about what it meant that he would restore "all things" (Mark 9:12).

❖ What do you think is the significance of the Transfiguration being so similar in nature to Moses' meeting with God on Mount Sinai?

_____

_____

_____

_____

_____

_____

Past to Present

Faulty Systems of Belief

Mark's first-century audience was only too well-acquainted with pain, insecurity, trials, and persecution. For them, the account of the Transfiguration—set in the midst of Jesus' teaching on the cost of discipleship—would have debunked any false hopes they had about reigning as kings and queens in their present world. Yet, at the same time, the account would have reaffirmed to them that Jesus—the one they served—was indeed the divine Son of God. It would also have also reassured them that one day they would be glorified with Jesus.

The Transfiguration provides the same lessons and assurances for us today. We, like Mark's first-century readers, are living in the time Jesus announced when he said that the time for the "kingdom of God has come near" (Mark 1:15). However, this doesn't mean we are reigning with Jesus on this earth or that suffering is a thing of the past. In this life, we still endure pain, insecurity, and trials—just like the early followers of Jesus. Yet we can take comfort in knowing that Jesus, the one we serve, is indeed the divine Son of God and that he has promised we will one day be glorified with him. We can know that our faith is built on a solid foundation.

❖ How does the story of the Transfiguration assure you that Jesus is the divine Son of God? In what ways does that give you hope today?

_____

_____

_____

_____

❖ How does this story in particular help you know that faith is built on a solid foundation? How can this help you get through the ups and downs of life?

_____

_____

_____

_____

_____

Life in the Valley

We all prefer the mountaintop experiences to those in the valley. We would rather spend our days on the mountain with the disciples, basking with them in the glory of the Lord, than down in the valleys serving his people and dealing with disgruntled crowds. Yet it is in the valleys below that we spend most of our lives. Earthly life cannot be lived primarily in heavenly visions.

God has work for each of us to do—and that work takes place down in the valleys. For this reason, we should cherish those times when we get to climb the mountain, and then hold on to the memories of the time we spent there. This life has a way of making us doubt whether those mountaintop experiences were real. We wonder if what we witnessed was just a mirage or hallucination. However, the words of our Lord remain constant. We must continue to listen to Jesus, whose words can sustain us when the visionary moments have grown dim.

❖ What are some of the spiritual mountaintop experiences you've had that stood out to you? Why were those times so meaningful?

_____

_____

_____

_____

❖ What are some of the spiritual valley experiences that you have gone through? How did you see God move even during those times?

_____

_____

_____

_____

_____

_____

Closing Prayer: *Jesus, I am ready to follow wherever you lead. Open my eyes to see you as you are—not as I want you to be. Speak truth where my thinking and perception are fuzzy. Grant me courage to take up the cross and lay my life down. Where I have created an image of you that is not accurate, speak your truth. Help me see you with such clarity that I follow you with all my heart, soul, mind, and strength. In your glorious name, amen.*

8

Faith in Action

Mark 9:14–29; 10:1–12, 17–31

In the 1800s, the Anglican clergyman William Bathurst penned a famous hymn in which he wrote, "Oh, for a faith that will not shrink, though pressed by every foe, that will not tremble on the brink of any earthly woe!" Bathurst went on to ask for a faith that "in the hour of grief or pain will lean upon its God" and "shines more bright and clear when tempests rage." His hymn captures the sentiment of the faith journey we find in Mark's Gospel.

Jesus knew the power of faith. As we saw in the previous lesson, when the woman with the issue of blood sought healing by touching the hem of his garment, he said to her, "Daughter, your faith has healed you. Go in peace and be freed from your suffering" (Mark 5:34). We also saw how Jesus "could not do any miracles" in his hometown of Nazareth because of the people's lack of faith (6:5). Yet Jesus was also patient with those who needed to increase their faith and allow it to transform their lives.

Faith is a gift from God, but it is also something that can grow and deepen as we exercise it. Jesus celebrates those who have faith and act on it. He delights when his followers step out in faith and operate in his power. He wants our faith to prompt us to take actions that are consistent with his will and change the world in profound ways.

Grow Your Faith [Mark 9:14–29]

¹⁴ When they came to the other disciples, they saw a large crowd around them and the teachers of the law arguing with them. ¹⁵ As soon as all the people saw Jesus, they were overwhelmed with wonder and ran to greet him.

¹⁶ "What are you arguing with them about?" he asked.

¹⁷ A man in the crowd answered, "Teacher, I brought you my son, who is possessed by a spirit that has robbed him of speech. ¹⁸ Whenever it seizes him, it throws him to the ground. He foams at the mouth, gnashes his teeth and becomes rigid. I asked your disciples to drive out the spirit, but they could not."

¹⁹ "You unbelieving generation," Jesus replied, "how long shall I stay with you? How long shall I put up with you? Bring the boy to me."

²⁰ So they brought him. When the spirit saw Jesus, it immediately threw the boy into a convulsion. He fell to the ground and rolled around, foaming at the mouth.

²¹ Jesus asked the boy's father, "How long has he been like this?"

"From childhood," he answered. ²² "It has often thrown him into fire or water to kill him. But if you can do anything, take pity on us and help us."

²³ "'If you can'?" said Jesus. "Everything is possible for one who believes."

²⁴ Immediately the boy's father exclaimed, "I do believe; help me overcome my unbelief!"

²⁵ When Jesus saw that a crowd was running to the scene, he rebuked the impure spirit. "You deaf and mute spirit," he said, "I command you, come out of him and never enter him again."

²⁶ The spirit shrieked, convulsed him violently and came out. The boy looked so much like a corpse that many said, "He's dead." ²⁷ But Jesus took him by the hand and lifted him to his feet, and he stood up.

²⁸ After Jesus had gone indoors, his disciples asked him privately, "Why couldn't we drive it out?"

²⁹ He replied, "This kind can come out only by prayer."

Original Meaning

At the heart of this story is not a struggle with a *demon* but a struggle for *faith*. The father has just witnessed the disciples fail in casting the demon out of his son—and must be wondering at this point if Jesus can do any better. Yet he has not lost all hope. His plea reveals that he does not doubt Jesus would *like* to do something but that he is uncertain whether Jesus *can* actually do anything. Jesus meets the father's skepticism with a question and a statement: "'If you can'? . . . Everything is possible for one who believes" (verse 23).

When Jesus singles out "one who believes," he has in mind both the miracle worker's faith and the faith of the one seeking the miracle. Jesus, as a miracle worker, possesses unlimited power because of his potent faith—and he does not want the father to put limits on what God can do to help him. Yet the petitioner also needs to possess faith in God. In this case, the faith of both Jesus and the father leads to success. Jesus rebukes the impure spirit and commands it to leave the boy.

Once the disciples are in the privacy of a house, they review their failure with Jesus. His response, "This kind can come out only by prayer" (verse 29), implies they failed because they had not prayed. However, Mark does not record Jesus offering up a specific prayer in this story to exorcise the unclean spirit. So what does he mean by "prayer" here? Most likely, what Jesus has in mind is a close relationship with the Father that comes through a life of prayer. We certainly see that Jesus had such a relationship with God (see Mark 1:35; 6:45–46).

❖ What do you learn in this story about the faith of the disciples, the faith of the demon-possessed boy's father, and the faith of Jesus?

Past to Present

Consider what this passage meant to the original readers and how it applies to us today.

The Need for Faith

The father in this story had almost reached the point where he had given up hope. It was there that Jesus met him and encouraged him to persevere. This is not to say Jesus expected the man to muster up a mighty faith before anything could be done. Rather, he wanted the father to trust that God could act decisively through him to heal his son. This kind of faith—though it might be small—had the potential to release great power in the man's life.

Faith requires humble trust on our part. Just like the father in this story, Jesus is not put off when we humbly and honesty come before him and say, "I believe . . . but I am not certain of it." He grants what is asked. Faith also comes as a gift from God and is sustained by the power of Jesus. Just as the father did not trust his own capacity to believe but asked for Jesus' help, so we must rely on Jesus to give us faith. The story that Mark presents thus reveals that God offers help not only for *healing* but also for increased *faith* in him.

❖ When is a time in your life where you sensed that God was calling you to "muster up" even a small amount of faith in him?

_____

_____

_____

_____

_____

_____

_____

_____

❖ How do you need Jesus to increase your faith in what he can do?

_____

_____

_____

_____

_____

_____

_____

The Need for Prayer

Jesus revealed the cause of the disciples' failure to heal the boy came about as a result of deficient faith and insufficient prayer. Today, it is easy for us to fall into the trap of believing we are too busy to pray or have too many things (even noble things) to do to spend time in prayer. We all too quickly treat prayer as a luxury and separate it from ministry. In reality, a life of prayer goes hand in hand with effective ministry.

When we are in close communion with God because of our regular habit of spending time with him, we will find it makes us receptive to the actions he performs in our midst. It is not possible to get ready for the moment when we need to see God's power at work by quickly uttering a "special" prayer. Rather, we have to be ready for when those moments arrive. This comes only through having a prayerful life with God.

❖ What are some of the things that get in the way of you spending time with Jesus? What would it take to get rid of those obstacles?

_____

_____

_____

_____

_____

_____

❖ How would you describe your prayer life with God? What would you say needs to improve?

_____

_____

_____

_____

A Question About Divorce [Mark 10:1–12]

¹ Jesus then left that place and went into the region of Judea and across the Jordan. Again crowds of people came to him, and as was his custom, he taught them.

² Some Pharisees came and tested him by asking, "Is it lawful for a man to divorce his wife?"

³ "What did Moses command you?" he replied.

⁴ They said, "Moses permitted a man to write a certificate of divorce and send her away."

⁵ "It was because your hearts were hard that Moses wrote you this law," Jesus replied. ⁶ "But at the beginning of creation God 'made them male and female.' ⁷ 'For this reason a man will leave his father and mother and be united to his wife, ⁸ and the two will become one flesh.' So they are no longer two, but one flesh. ⁹ Therefore what God has joined together, let no one separate."

¹⁰ When they were in the house again, the disciples asked Jesus about this. ¹¹ He answered, "Anyone who divorces his wife and marries another woman commits adultery against her. ¹² And if she divorces her husband and marries another man, she commits adultery."

Original Meaning

The Pharisees in this story are interested in more than just Jesus' legal opinion about divorce. Mark states they want to "test" Jesus, which indicates they were hoping to provoke him into saying something that would put him at odds with the crowd. Jesus fends off their attack by asking, "What did Moses *command* you?" (verse 3, emphasis added). The Pharisees were looking to see what the law would *allow* them to do. Jesus recast the question from a hypothetical debate about some unspecified husband to a command from Moses directed at them.

The Pharisees respond by citing the Mosaic regulations regarding divorce: Moses *permitted* it, provided the husband gave his wife a certificate of divorce (see Deuteronomy 24:1–4). The law does not outline the grounds for divorce nor endorse it—it simply places restrictions on the husband should he decide to do it. Jesus responds by stating that what Moses commanded was only a compromise intended to reduce the fallout from men's hardness of heart. The law kept the upheaval associated with divorce to a minimum.

Jesus goes on to say that God's original plans for husbands and wives can be found at the beginning of creation: "A man leaves his father and mother and is united to his wife, and they become one flesh" (Genesis 2:24). Divorce does not reflect God's will. What is important is not what Moses *permitted* because of people's sin but what God *commands*.

❖ What was Jesus attempting to reveal to the Pharisees about their heart toward God and their heart toward other people?

Past to Present

No Escape Clauses

Jesus proclaimed throughout Mark's Gospel that the kingdom of God was breaking into the world and into people's lives. He told creative stories and parables to help his followers imagine what this meant in their lives. Similarly, this has direct implications for how we should live. We can no longer deal with God based on what Moses may have "permitted." Rather, God's will must invade all areas of our lives, including what is culturally accepted and legally allowed. Jesus makes *radical* demands of his disciples. He calls us to put ourselves last by serving others and to be willing to sacrifice for them—and these commands also apply to marriage. We cannot simply search through the Bible and look for escape clauses that match our particular situation. We must instead seek to discern the will of God as we study Scripture.

❖ What does it mean to you that God's will must invade *all* areas of your life?

_____

_____

_____

❖ Jesus calls you to put others first and be willing to sacrifice for them. How does this apply to your closest relationships (marriage, children, parents, friendships)?

_____

_____

_____

Riches and Faith [Mark 10:17–31]

¹⁷ As Jesus started on his way, a man ran up to him and fell on his knees before him. "Good teacher," he asked, "what must I do to inherit eternal life?"
¹⁸ "Why do you call me good?" Jesus answered. "No one is good—except God alone. ¹⁹ You know the commandments: 'You shall not murder,

you shall not commit adultery, you shall not steal, you shall not give false testimony, you shall not defraud, honor your father and mother.'"

20 "Teacher," he declared, "all these I have kept since I was a boy."

21 Jesus looked at him and loved him. "One thing you lack," he said. "Go, sell everything you have and give to the poor, and you will have treasure in heaven. Then come, follow me."

22 At this the man's face fell. He went away sad, because he had great wealth.

23 Jesus looked around and said to his disciples, "How hard it is for the rich to enter the kingdom of God!"

24 The disciples were amazed at his words. But Jesus said again, "Children, how hard it is to enter the kingdom of God! 25 It is easier for a camel to go through the eye of a needle than for someone who is rich to enter the kingdom of God."

26 The disciples were even more amazed, and said to each other, "Who then can be saved?"

27 Jesus looked at them and said, "With man this is impossible, but not with God; all things are possible with God."

28 Then Peter spoke up, "We have left everything to follow you!"

29 "Truly I tell you," Jesus replied, "no one who has left home or brothers or sisters or mother or father or children or fields for me and the gospel 30 will fail to receive a hundred times as much in this present age: homes, brothers, sisters, mothers, children and fields—along with persecutions—and in the age to come eternal life. 31 But many who are first will be last, and the last first."

Original Meaning

The Jewish man who falls on his knees before Jesus addresses him as "good teacher." The Jewish readers of Mark's Gospel might have expected Jesus to respond according to custom with equally exalted language: "Most honored and good sir." Instead, Jesus addresses him with no title at all and corrects him in thinking that anyone other than God is good.

Jesus then directs the man to the Ten Commandments. The man replies that he has kept all these since he was a boy—and Jesus does not sneer at his claims. Instead, he gives the man a direct challenge. If he truly wants to secure treasure in *heaven*, then he needs to sell all that he has on *earth* and give it to the poor. It is then that Mark reveals this man had great wealth. His unhappy departure reveals that he does not want to enter life under Jesus' guidance. However, Jesus will not negotiate terms with those who want to be his disciples.

This encounter teaches that Jesus requires more from his disciples than reverence for him as a good teacher and earnest attempts to obey God's commands. Entering into God's kingdom requires submitting to his rule and allowing him to reign over every aspect of life. Those who are ruled by money thus cannot be ruled by God. Peter is quick to remind Jesus that he and the other disciples have done exactly that—they have left everything to follow him. Jesus promises them, just as he promises us, that such sacrifice will not be for naught.

❖ What did Jesus mean when he said it is hard for the rich to enter the kingdom of God? Why might this statement have sparked amazement in the disciples?

_____

_____

_____

_____

Past to Present

Trust in God

The man in this story told Jesus that he had kept all the commandments since he was a boy. Still, Jesus said, there was *one thing* that he lacked. Jesus didn't specify what that "one thing" was, but we can surmise that he lacked at least two things, beginning with *trust in God*. The man had wealth and all that came with it—honor, respect, power—but this did not make him holy or grant him eternal life. He wanted to serve God on his own terms . . . obeying the commandments that suited him but resisting turning his whole life over to God.

God requires more from us than simply reverence for Jesus and zealous attempts at obedience. He wants us to completely put our trust in him and depend on him for our every need. Money and possessions provide a false sense of security because we fall into the mindset that if we have enough wealth, we will be able to cover our losses when the storms of life come. What God is asking us to do is give up the quest to create our own security, which, in the end, proves to be a false security. God wants us to let go of the safety net and trust that he will catch us. When we do this, we witness the incredible ways that God works in our lives.

❖ In what ways have you seen money create a false sense of security in people?

_____

_____

_____

_____

❖ How would you describe your attitude toward money? What is a "safety net" you have created that God is asking you to release?

_____

_____

_____

_____

_____

Compassion for Others

The second thing the wealthy man lacked was *compassion for others*. He was unwilling to give what he possessed for the benefit of others because he was preoccupied with himself. He asked, "What must *I* do to inherit eternal life" (verse 17, emphasis added) and "went away sad" (verse 22) when Jesus told him to give to the poor. This attitude was completely at odds with Jesus, who had compassion on the crowds and met their needs. It was also completely at odds with what Jesus said those who desired to be his disciples must do. Wealth can blind our moral judgment, harden the arteries of our compassion, and lead to spiritual bankruptcy. It can create an "us versus them" mentality where we distance ourselves from those who do not have what we possess. Jesus commands us to let go of this attitude and learn what it means to love others.

❖ What are some of the ways you use your God-given resources to help others in need?

_____

_____

_____

_____

❖ How would you like God to increase your compassion for others?

_____

_____

_____

_____

Closing Prayer: Lord, help me where I need deeper faith in you. Spare me from the folly of faith that has no action. Make my faith so deep that it moves me to live for you, follow you, love others well, and serve those in need. Help me to view my possessions not as security in this world but as gifts from you to be used for your kingdom. In your name, amen.

9

What Matters Most

Mark 10:32-45; 11:1-11, 12-25

Position. Prestige. Power. Possessions. Popularity. These are some of the things the world whispers should matter the most to you. *You need a good position where you work so people will look up to you. You need prestige so people will respect you. You need power so people will obey you. You need possessions so people will want to be just like you. You need popularity so people will want to be around you.* It is so easy to listen to these whispers. Before you know it, you are drawn into seeking after these things with all your heart.

When we think about the disciples, we don't often consider the personality clashes and power struggles that occurred among them. The disciples came from all different walks of life, so we can assume they frequently did not see eye to eye on things. Peter, in particular, appears to have been quite impetuous and brash at times. Yet he was alone in this, for as we will see in this section in Mark, the disciples James and John could also make outlandish requests of Jesus—particularly when it came to what their rank would be in God's future kingdom.

Shockingly, this request came immediately after Jesus told his disciples that he was about to be arrested by the religious leaders in Jerusalem and be condemned to death. Jesus, who held all authority and power, was about to willingly give up his life for the sins of the world. Meanwhile, his disciples were squabbling about who was the greatest among them! It is a great lesson for us today when it comes to considering what matters most. Do we value the things of God the most? Or are our hearts more set on chasing after the things of the world?

A Power Struggle in the Ranks [Mark 10:32-45]

32 They were on their way up to Jerusalem, with Jesus leading the way, and the disciples were astonished, while those who followed were afraid. Again he took the Twelve aside and told them what was going to happen to him. 33 "We are going up to Jerusalem," he said, "and the Son of Man will be delivered over to the chief priests and the teachers of the law. They will condemn him to death and will hand him over to the Gentiles, 34 who will mock him and spit on him, flog him and kill him. Three days later he will rise."

35 Then James and John, the sons of Zebedee, came to him. "Teacher," they said, "we want you to do for us whatever we ask."

36 "What do you want me to do for you?" he asked.

37 They replied, "Let one of us sit at your right and the other at your left in your glory."

38 "You don't know what you are asking," Jesus said. "Can you drink the cup I drink or be baptized with the baptism I am baptized with?"

39 "We can," they answered.

Jesus said to them, "You will drink the cup I drink and be baptized with the baptism I am baptized with, 40 but to sit at my right or left is not for me to grant. These places belong to those for whom they have been prepared."

41 When the ten heard about this, they became indignant with James and John. 42 Jesus called them together and said, "You know that those who are regarded as rulers of the Gentiles lord it over them, and their high officials exercise authority over them. 43 Not so with you. Instead, whoever wants to become great among you must be your servant, 44 and whoever wants to be first must be slave of all. 45 For even the Son of Man did not come to be served, but to serve, and to give his life as a ransom for many."

Original Meaning

Mark now reveals where Jesus and his disciples are headed: Jerusalem. Jesus is going there as the Messiah who will invite all Israel to come under God's mysterious dominion. Yet as Jesus draws nearer to his ordeal, the disciples do not draw nearer in understanding. Jesus, for the third time in Mark's Gospel, speaks to them about his suffering, death, and resurrection. Once again, his words go in one ear and out the other.

Immediately after the announcement, James and John approach Jesus with a request. The earlier dispute about rank among the disciples (see Mark 9:34) was silenced but not buried. Just like Peter, the two misinterpret what it means for Jesus to be the Messiah and assume that when he ushers in the new age, they will receive special privileges.

Jesus responds to their selfish request with grace. He asks whether they can drink from the cup he drinks—a metaphor for suffering (see Isaiah 51:17)—and be baptized with the baptism he will endure—a metaphor for being plunged into calamity (see Psalm 42:7). In other words, are they willing to share his fate and be doused with the waters of trial? James and John are as overconfident in their own abilities as was the rich man. Furthermore, Jesus informs them the Father has not placed him in charge of the seating arrangements in the kingdom.

The other disciples are livid at the request. This is not because James and John have been so insensitive but because they have beat them to the punch. Now they might have an edge over them for the power slots. The disciples would rather bear a grudge than a cross!

❖ What does the request of James and John indicate about where their minds were in considering Jesus to be the Messiah?

Past to Present

Consider what this passage meant to the original readers and how it applies to us today.

Keep Your Ambitions in Check

Mark's original readers would have been struck by how the disciples were once again competing for first place. They wanted to dominate one another rather than serve each other. They desired for Jesus to be a Messiah who would offer them all their heart's desires and positions of privilege. They certainly did not expect a Messiah who would suffer and die. However, according to Mark, we can never understand who Jesus is without understanding the necessity of his final destiny of suffering.

Following Jesus requires us to keep our ambitions in check. It demands that we share in his self-giving love, service, and suffering before we can share in his glory (see Romans 8:17). All too frequently, we fall into the world's way of thinking that we should always seek to better ourselves in this life no matter what the cost might be to others. Even the church has to endure power struggles that make it look no different from the corporate world. God calls us to lay aside such grabs for worldly power and pursue his kingdom. As James instructed, "Humble yourselves before the Lord, and he will lift you up" (James 4:10).

❖ What does it mean for you personally to share in Jesus' self-giving love, service, and suffering? How does that type of heart attitude show up in your life?

_____

_____

_____

_____

❖ What are some ways you seek to keep your ambitions in check? What can you identify as some of the dreams and goals that *God* has given to you?

_____

_____

_____

_____

_____

Keep Your Requests in Check

This scene in Mark's Gospel should cause each of us to reexamine our requests to God. It is striking that James and John made such a bold request for power *immediately* after Jesus had told them about his upcoming suffering and death. Even the way the two disciples phrased the request should give us pause: "Teacher . . . we want you to do for us whatever we ask" (verse 35). It was almost as if they were asking Jesus to sign a blank check!

We can all see ourselves in James and John. After all, how many of us have asked God for promotions at work, bigger cars, and all sorts of other personal advancements? The disciples' selfish request so often matches our own. Meanwhile, Jesus is saying to us—just as he said to his twelve disciples—"whoever wants to become great among you must be your servant," and "whoever wants to be first must be slave of all" (verses 43–44).

❖ When you consider your prayers, what type of requests do you make the most often? How many of your requests are for yourself, and how many are for others?

_____

_____

_____

_____

❖ How often do you pray to be a part of what God is doing in this world? What does this story reveal to you about the kind of requests God wants you to make?

_____

_____

_____

_____

_____

The True King Comes to Jerusalem [Mark 11:1-11]

¹ As they approached Jerusalem and came to Bethphage and Bethany at the Mount of Olives, Jesus sent two of his disciples, ² saying to them, "Go to the village ahead of you, and just as you enter it, you will find a colt tied there, which no one has ever ridden. Untie it and bring it here. ³ If anyone asks you, 'Why are you doing this?' say, 'The Lord needs it and will send it back here shortly.'"

⁴ They went and found a colt outside in the street, tied at a doorway. As they untied it, ⁵ some people standing there asked, "What are you doing, untying that colt?" ⁶ They answered as Jesus had told them to, and the people let them go. ⁷ When they brought the colt to Jesus and threw their cloaks over it, he sat on it. ⁸ Many people spread their cloaks on the road, while others spread branches they had cut in the fields. ⁹ Those who went ahead and those who followed shouted,

"Hosanna!"

"Blessed is he who comes in the name of the Lord!"

¹⁰ "Blessed is the coming kingdom of our father David!"

"Hosanna in the highest heaven!"

¹¹ Jesus entered Jerusalem and went into the temple courts. He looked around at everything, but since it was already late, he went out to Bethany with the Twelve.

Original Meaning

Mark's readers would have noticed in this story that Jesus has departed from his previous patterns of movement. Up to this point, he has walked everywhere, except for the times he crossed the lake in a boat. Now he rides a colt that has never been ridden—which, in those times, made it worthy of a king. Jesus' entry into Jerusalem also deviates from his previous patterns of not calling attention to himself. What we observe now is actually a complete reversal: Jesus *encourages* public rejoicing through his provocative entrance.

The excitement generated by Jesus' arrival ends somewhat anticlimactically when he enters the temple, looks around, and leaves. Mark raises his readers' expectations that something grand will happen . . . but nothing does. He writes that "it was already late" (verse 11), but late for what? Did time run out on Jesus before he could do anything? Or is time running out for the temple? This colorless ending to Jesus' dramatic entry into Jerusalem reveals more than meets the eye. Jesus enters the temple to inspect it. The next day's events will reveal that he comes not to restore it but to pronounce God's judgment on it.

❖ How does Jesus present himself to the people as he enters Jerusalem? What makes his arrival noteworthy?

Past to Present

The Salvation Jesus Offers

The crowd is mistaken in their acclaim of Jesus. They treat his approach as a triumphal entry and shout nationalist slogans about the restoration of the Davidic kingdom. They are right that Jesus comes as a king, but they expect him to be a typical monarch who will establish a temporal empire. They wrongly presume that Jesus is entering Jerusalem to purge the nation of Roman domination and bring back the ancient glories of Israel in the days of David.

What the people actually needed—and what we need—is for Jesus to save them from themselves. Human nature changes little over the years, and this incident reveals that we still need saving. We need to be saved from the petty nationalism that divides our world into tiny enclaves set against one another. Jesus came as the king over the entire world and died for all people. We need to be saved from weak faith that abandons Jesus at the first sign of trouble. The throngs who cheered Jesus' arrival would not be there a few days later when he faced suffering. Jesus wants those who will endure with him to the end.

❖ Jesus was not the kind of king the people were expecting. When has Jesus shown up in your life in a way you did not expect? How has he revealed himself as king to you?

_____

_____

_____

❖ When you look at the world today, what kind of "saving" needs to take place? Where do you most desire Jesus to make his power known as the king over your life?

_____

_____

_____

The Temple Action [Mark 11:12–25]

¹² The next day as they were leaving Bethany, Jesus was hungry. ¹³ Seeing in the distance a fig tree in leaf, he went to find out if it had any fruit. When

he reached it, he found nothing but leaves, because it was not the season for figs. ¹⁴ Then he said to the tree, "May no one ever eat fruit from you again." And his disciples heard him say it.

¹⁵ On reaching Jerusalem, Jesus entered the temple courts and began driving out those who were buying and selling there. He overturned the tables of the money changers and the benches of those selling doves, ¹⁶ and would not allow anyone to carry merchandise through the temple courts. ¹⁷ And as he taught them, he said, "Is it not written: 'My house will be called a house of prayer for all nations'? But you have made it 'a den of robbers.'"

¹⁸ The chief priests and the teachers of the law heard this and began looking for a way to kill him, for they feared him, because the whole crowd was amazed at his teaching.

¹⁹ When evening came, Jesus and his disciples went out of the city.

²⁰ In the morning, as they went along, they saw the fig tree withered from the roots. ²¹ Peter remembered and said to Jesus, "Rabbi, look! The fig tree you cursed has withered!"

²² "Have faith in God," Jesus answered. ²³ "Truly I tell you, if anyone says to this mountain, 'Go, throw yourself into the sea,' and does not doubt in their heart but believes that what they say will happen, it will be done for them. ²⁴ Therefore I tell you, whatever you ask for in prayer, believe that you have received it, and it will be yours. ²⁵ And when you stand praying, if you hold anything against anyone, forgive them, so that your Father in heaven may forgive you your sins."

Original Meaning

The temple in Jerusalem had become a nationalistic symbol in Jesus' day that only served to divide Israel from the other nations. If it were to become what God intended, "a house of prayer for all nations" (verse 17), then walls would have to crumble. Indeed, this would soon happen when Jesus died on the cross and the temple veil was split from top to bottom (see Mark 15:38–39).

Jesus describes the temple as "a den of robbers" (verse 17). The statement has nothing to do with the trade going on there but is instead a reference to a prophecy in Jeremiah 7:1–15. Jesus is proclaiming that the same abuses that sullied the temple in the prophet Jeremiah's time are still tainting it now. The temple has become a hiding place where the religious think they can find forgiveness and fellowship with God no matter how they act on the outside. It has become a sanctuary for bandits who think they are protected from God's judgment.

Mark sandwiches the temple incident around a narrative about a fig tree, which indicates that both episodes are to be interpreted together. In truth, the cursing of the fig tree helps to explain what Jesus does in the temple. It reveals that Jesus' intention is not to *cleanse* the temple but to announce its *disqualification*. The fig tree that has not borne fruit is cursed rather than reformed. The barrenness of the plant represents the barrenness of those in temple Judaism who are unprepared to accept Jesus' messianic reign.

❖ What issues about the "religious" was Jesus calling out?

_____

_____

_____

_____

Past to Present

Breaking Systems of Power

Jesus' denouncement of the temple was also a denouncement of the corrupt system of domination that had developed among God's people. The temple had become a center of power for the nobility who dominated, controlled, indoctrinated, and exploited those who ranked lower on the social scale. The thinking of the day held that people were poor, suffering, and oppressed because they had sinned against God. For people to be forgiven, they had to offer a sacrifice, which ultimately lined the pockets of those primarily responsible for oppressing the poor. This was not God's original intention for the temple, but human corruption had taken over.

When Jesus pronounced that "the Son of Man has authority on earth to forgive sins" (Mark 2:10), he bypassed this corrupt system and subverted it. Today, Jesus calls each of us to likewise break down systems of injustice in our world—systems that oppress people and hold them down. As he proclaimed in Luke's Gospel at the start of his ministry: "The Spirit of the Lord is on me, because he has anointed me to proclaim good news to the poor. He has sent me to proclaim freedom for the prisoners and recovery of sight for the blind, to set the oppressed free, to proclaim the year of the Lord's favor" (Luke 4:18–19).

❖ What are some oppressive systems of power that you have seen in the world? Have you witnessed oppressive systems of power in the church?

_____

_____

_____

_____

❖ How do you stand up against injustice when you see it?

_____

_____

_____

_____

A Community of Prayer

The Jewish people regarded the temple as the place of prayer. In fact, as Jesus stated, the temple was supposed to be a house of prayer for all nations. However, in his explanation of the fig tree's withering, he envisioned a future without a temple. Yet the demise of the temple would not bring an end to effective prayer. Instead, the existing religious establishment would be replaced by a kingdom community whose power lay in faith-borne prayer.

We are members of this community. So what should prayer look like for us? First, we *pray receptively*. Prayer is not imposing our will on God but opening up our lives to his will. Second, we *pray confidently*. We pray in Jesus' name, confident of God's response, knowing that what we seek is compatible with Jesus' teaching, life, and death. We *pray expectantly*. Our prayers focus not only on our little world and our immediate future but also on the long-term and the large scale: "Your kingdom come, your will be done" (Matthew 6:10). Finally, we pray with a *forgiving spirit*. We make peace with others so we can be at peace with God.

❖ Why is it important to pray receptively and confidently? What does it mean for you to open yourself up to God's will when you pray?

_____

_____

_____

❖ Why is it important for you to pray expectantly and with a forgiving spirit? How does praying in these ways help you to focus on others more than on yourself?

_____

_____

_____

Closing Prayer: God of wisdom and truth, speak to me today and show me what matters most. Search my heart and reveal where my priorities are skewed and my goals are selfish. Spirit of the living God, give me power to prioritize my life around your will, your ways, and your Word. Make what matters most to you the consuming passion of my life. Amen.

10

Instructions
and Warnings

Mark 12:1-12, 28-34; 13:1-13

Picture the scene. You and your spouse have decided to go out for dinner and a movie by yourselves. It will be the first time you will leave your oldest teenage child in charge while you are gone. (If you are not married and/or do not have kids, just play along!)

What will you do?

Well, if you are like most parents, you will give your children instructions to follow while you are out and warnings of things to watch for as they wait for you to return.

In this next section of Mark, we find Jesus doing the same. Except, in this case, he is preparing his twelve *disciples* for when he will leave this world. It begins with Jesus following his typical pattern for teaching by telling a parable. However, this parable is different in that Jesus uses it to tell of his own rejection by the religious leaders and his death. What follows is a lesson to his followers about what they should be doing while he is gone: *loving* one another.

Jesus also presents a whole series of warnings for his disciples. He informs them of deceivers who will come in his name. He tells of wars and rumors of wars. He prepares them for the scorn and trials they will endure for remaining true to him—the exact kind of persecution that

Mark's readers were now facing because of their faith. Believers in *every generation* need to hear these words and take them to heart until the day Jesus returns in glory.

Parable of the Tenants [Mark 12:1-12]

[1] Jesus then began to speak to them in parables: "A man planted a vineyard. He put a wall around it, dug a pit for the winepress and built a watchtower. Then he rented the vineyard to some farmers and moved to another place. [2] At harvest time he sent a servant to the tenants to collect from them some of the fruit of the vineyard. [3] But they seized him, beat him and sent him away empty-handed. [4] Then he sent another servant to them; they struck this man on the head and treated him shamefully. [5] He sent still another, and that one they killed. He sent many others; some of them they beat, others they killed.

[6] "He had one left to send, a son, whom he loved. He sent him last of all, saying, 'They will respect my son.'

[7] "But the tenants said to one another, 'This is the heir. Come, let's kill him, and the inheritance will be ours.' [8] So they took him and killed him, and threw him out of the vineyard.

[9] "What then will the owner of the vineyard do? He will come and kill those tenants and give the vineyard to others. [10] Haven't you read this passage of Scripture:

"'The stone the builders rejected
has become the cornerstone;
[11] the Lord has done this,
and it is marvelous in our eyes'?"

[12] Then the chief priests, the teachers of the law and the elders looked for a way to arrest him because they knew he had spoken the parable against them. But they were afraid of the crowd; so they left him and went away.

Original Meaning

The parable that Jesus tells in this section of Mark is directed at the chief priests, teachers of the law, and elders (see Mark 11:27). Given these leaders' hostility, what happens to Jesus—the vineyard owner's son—comes as no surprise. Yet the parable allows Mark's readers to see these events from the perspective of God's long and turbulent relationship with Israel.

In the story, the vineyard owner sends his *servants* to the tenants. In the Old Testament, the term *servant* was frequently used for the prophets that God sent to his people. The servants' treatment in the allegory surely calls to mind the ill treatment of the prophets—and the abuse these servants receive progressively becomes worse. Finally, "last of all," the owner sent "a son, whom he loved" (verse 6), which recalls the voice from heaven identifying Jesus as "my Son, whom I love" (1:11). The son's mission is the same as that of the servants.

The tenants recognize the son as the heir and desire to get his inheritance for themselves. They assassinate the son, throw his body outside, and leave him there unburied. In that day and age, to refuse to bury a corpse would have been seen as an incredible offense. Jesus concludes the parable with a question: "What then will the owner of the vineyard do?" (verse 9). He does not wait for an answer but gives it himself. The Lord of the vineyard will destroy the tenants who killed his servants and son and give the vineyard to others.

Jesus closes the confrontation with a citation from Psalm 118:22–23—the psalm the crowd chanted when he entered Jerusalem earlier that week. The stone the builders discarded becomes the cornerstone of a new structure, implying a new temple. Mark's readers would have understood that Jesus was saying that he is the stone of stumbling the psalmist spoke about. The parable thus reflects Jesus' full consciousness of his sonship in relation to the vineyard owner and his awareness of his impending death at the hands of the authorities.

❖ How do the chief priests, teachers of the law, and elders respond to Jesus' parable? Why do you think they respond in this way?

_____

_____

_____

_____

Past to Present

A Rebellious Nature

In considering how the parable applies to us today, we need to look at the primary characters in the story. The tenants live in a self-centered, cutthroat world with no awareness or respect toward the vineyard owner. When the lord sent his servants to secure some of the harvest from his own vineyard, they refused to part with any of the fruits of their labor. The tenants wanted to establish *themselves* as lords of their own little worlds. The owner, however, stood in the way of their self-absorbed plans. Their defiance only secured their final destruction.

The psalmist wrote, "The earth is the LORD's, and everything in it" (Psalm 24:1). We may fall into the trap of thinking we run the show and are in control of our own little worlds, but the reality is that the Lord sees all and has authority over all. He may seem like an absentee landlord to us, but the truth is that he is ever present in our lives. When he steps into our lives and asks us to give of ourselves for the work of his kingdom, we should heed his call. If we do not, we face the same prospects of judgment from God that the tenants faced.

❖ In what ways can you see yourself in the tenants in this parable?

_____

_____

_____

❖ How has God has revealed that *he* is the one in charge of your life?

_____

_____

_____

_____

A Loving Nature

The vineyard owner would not allow his tenants to live in their rebellion without sending servants to warn them of the consequences. He gave the tenants ample time and opportunity to repent—sending his servants repeatedly to compel them to change their ways. But the tenants only responded by beating or killing the servants their lord had mercifully sent to them. Finally, as a last attempt, the owner sent his own son. When the tenants killed him, the owner had no recourse but to allow them to suffer the judgment they so richly deserved.

The Lord is loving toward us. He wants us to come to repentance and seek the salvation he made available to us through the teachings, death, and resurrection of his Son. Peter wrote, "The Lord . . . is patient with you, not wanting anyone to perish, but everyone to come to repentance" (2 Peter 3:9). He gives us ample opportunities to come to him and change our ways. Our part is to grasp hold of the mercy he extends to us, accept his offer of salvation, and then change our ways. In this way, we can avoid the fate of the wicked tenants in the story.

❖ How has the Lord demonstrated his patience toward you when it comes to repentance?

_____

_____

_____

_____

_____

❖ What acts of mercy are you grateful for God extending to you? Why do those particular acts from the Lord stand out to you?

_____

_____

_____

_____

The Greatest Commandment [Mark 12:28–34]

28 One of the teachers of the law came and heard them debating. Noticing that Jesus had given them a good answer, he asked him, "Of all the commandments, which is the most important?"

29 "The most important one," answered Jesus, "is this: 'Hear, O Israel: The Lord our God, the Lord is one. 30 Love the Lord your God with all your heart and with all your soul and with all your mind and with all your strength.' 31 The second is this: 'Love your neighbor as yourself.' There is no commandment greater than these."

32 "Well said, teacher," the man replied. "You are right in saying that God is one and there is no other but him. 33 To love him with all your heart, with all your understanding and with all your strength, and to love your neighbor as yourself is more important than all burnt offerings and sacrifices."

34 When Jesus saw that he had answered wisely, he said to him, "You are not far from the kingdom of God." And from then on no one dared ask him any more questions.

Original Meaning

In this scene, a teacher of the law comes to Jesus and prods him with another question: "Of all the commandments, which is the most important?" (verse 28). Mark's Jewish readers would have seen that the teacher assumes there is a distinction among the 613 commands in God's law—248 of which are positive commands and 365 of which are prohibitions.

Some of these commands were considered to be lighter (smaller) and some weightier (greater).

The teacher is looking for Jesus to comment on what is the *fundamental premise* of the law on which the individual commands depend. The reply Jesus gives is from the daily confession of Israel known as the *Shema*—that God is the only God and one is to love him with one's whole being: heart, soul, mind, and strength (see Deuteronomy 6:4–9). Jesus then couples this command to love God with the command to love one's neighbor as oneself (see Leviticus 19:18). A person cannot love God in isolation from other relationships in life. Love is our inner commitment to God that is expressed in all our conduct and relationships.

The teacher of the law affirms that Jesus has answered his question well. He adds that to do these things "is more important than all burnt offerings and sacrifices" (verse 33). In this way, he reinforces for Mark's readers that the temple is now irrelevant for fulfilling God's most vital demands. When people truly extend love for God and for others, they have offered the one sacrifice that is well pleasing to God. The affirmation also reveals that those who believe Jesus is the Messiah are not deviating from the fundamental core of Jewish beliefs.

❖ Why do you think Jesus said this teacher of the law was "not far from the kingdom of God" after giving his response?

Past to Present

Loving God with Heart and Soul
We can't just worship God for a few minutes in church each week and then ignore him in the rest of our lives—at work, at home, or at play. God

wants us to love him at all times *with all our heart*. In the Bible, the *heart* is the command center of the body, where decisions are made and plans are formed. It is the center of our inner being, which controls our feelings, emotions, desires, and passions. The heart is where religious commitment takes root.

God also desires us to love him *with all our soul*. God gave breath to the soul of humans (see Genesis 2:7). The *soul* is the source of vitality in life (see Job 33:4). It is the motivating power that brings strength of will. Along with the heart, the soul determines conduct. When we are commanded to love God with all our soul, it refers to the power of our lives. When we love God with all our soul, we commit all our energy and strength to him.

❖ What does it mean to love God with all your heart? How can you tell when your heart-love for God is waning?

_____

_____

_____

_____

❖ What tends to deplete the power source of your love for God? How do you tend to your soul so you can avoid this happening?

_____

_____

_____

_____

Loving God with Mind and Strength

Jesus also states that we are to love God *with all our mind*. The mind is the faculty of perception and reflection that directs our opinions and judgments. Our love for God requires more than an emotional response or a swirl of activity in God's name. We are to love God with our *intelligence*. God does not want us to check out intellectually when we enter into worship. Rather, he desires for us to engage our faith by actively engaging our minds.

Furthermore, we must love God *with all our strength*. The term *strength* refers to our physical capacities and includes our possessions. Mark relates a story shortly after Jesus' teaching on the greatest commandment of a poor widow putting a few small copper coins into the temple treasury. Meanwhile, the rich gave what they skimmed off the top of their abundance. Jesus commended the woman because she loved God with all her strength. She gave a tithe out of her lack and did not worry about what would be left over (see Mark 12:41–44).

❖ What helps you to keep your mind on Jesus and on the things of God? What tends to distract your thinking and make you focus on less important things?

_____

_____

_____

_____

❖ What are some practical ways you demonstrate your love to God through how you use the resources he has given to you? How does this help you trust in God's provision?

_____

_____

_____

_____

Final Warnings [Mark 13:1–13]

[1] As Jesus was leaving the temple, one of his disciples said to him, "Look, Teacher! What massive stones! What magnificent buildings!"

² "Do you see all these great buildings?" replied Jesus. "Not one stone here will be left on another; every one will be thrown down."

³ As Jesus was sitting on the Mount of Olives opposite the temple, Peter, James, John and Andrew asked him privately, ⁴ "Tell us, when will these things happen? And what will be the sign that they are all about to be fulfilled?"

⁵ Jesus said to them: "Watch out that no one deceives you. ⁶ Many will come in my name, claiming, 'I am he,' and will deceive many. ⁷ When you hear of wars and rumors of wars, do not be alarmed. Such things must happen, but the end is still to come. ⁸ Nation will rise against nation, and kingdom against kingdom. There will be earthquakes in various places, and famines. These are the beginning of birth pains.

⁹ "You must be on your guard. You will be handed over to the local councils and flogged in the synagogues. On account of me you will stand before governors and kings as witnesses to them. ¹⁰ And the gospel must first be preached to all nations. ¹¹ Whenever you are arrested and brought to trial, do not worry beforehand about what to say. Just say whatever is given you at the time, for it is not you speaking, but the Holy Spirit.

¹² "Brother will betray brother to death, and a father his child. Children will rebel against their parents and have them put to death. ¹³ Everyone will hate you because of me, but the one who stands firm to the end will be saved.

Original Meaning

As Jesus departs the temple, the disciples look back and are awed by its magnificence. Early writers report that the temple was covered with plates of gold that reflected the rays of the sun and made people look away due to its brightness. The stone used in the temple's construction was a pale limestone that made it appear from a distance like a mountain covered with snow. Yet Jesus says to his disciples that not one of those majestic stones will be left on another.

What has been implicit in Jesus' actions in the temple now becomes explicit. He openly prophesies its complete destruction. The statement prompts Peter, James, John, and Andrew to ask exactly when this will occur and what the signs will be so they can be prepared. Jesus responds by giving them several clues—the theme of which is that they should not be deceived by events or by false prophets. He tells them that deceivers will lay claim to divine authority that belongs only to him. These messianic pretenders will dupe many with their daring declarations, but the disciples must not be caught up in the delusions of the crowd.

Jesus also warns about international commotions, natural disasters, and persecutions. He identifies these as the "beginning of birth pains" (verse 8)—a time of suffering. These persecutions will single out followers of Jesus for persecution simply because they follow him. So, when these things happen, astute disciples will recognize they are suffering precisely what their Lord prophesied. They will suffer what Jesus himself endured. In the midst of this bleak landscape, the one bright light is God's intention to get the word of the gospel out to all. The gospel must first be preached to all nations before these things occur.

❖ What did Jesus promise would happen when his followers were arrested? What is the promise for those who remain faithful to him?

_____

_____

_____

Past to Present

Preach the Gospel

Jesus reveals what must happen before the end comes, but he does not give precise dates or details. This is because God has not revealed it even to him (see Mark 13:32). Of course, this has not stopped people from making predictions—and then revising the dates and descriptions of what they predicted when they don't pan out. This is ironic, given that Jesus warns us against engaging in any eschatological hysteria.

It is significant that in the midst of Jesus' descriptions and warnings of these events, he calls his followers to *preach the gospel* to all nations. Jesus' primary focus is not for his disciples to know exactly when the endtimes will come but for them to know *what they should be doing* as they wait for his return. We may live in times of persecution and natural disasters, or we may experience relative comfort and peace. Whichever it is, Jesus requires unceasing vigilance so we remain spiritually alert even when everything seems to indicate there is peace and safety.

❖ What emotions stir in you when you read Jesus' descriptions of the endtimes and what will happen?

_____

_____

_____

❖ In what ways are you "preaching the gospel" to your corner of the world in word and deed? What else do you sense that Jesus is calling you to do as you wait for his return?

_____

_____

_____

Closing Prayer: Jesus, give me spiritual insight to see when human systems are taking precedence over my devotion to you. Forgive me for those times when I allow the things of the world to grab my attention and devotion more than your Word and the leading of your Holy Spirit. Help me to seek first your kingdom and your righteousness. You alone are on the throne of my life. Amen.

11

The Countdown Commences

Mark 14:1-11, 17-31, 32-50

Many popular sporting events today depend on the use of a device that is so common we often overlook it. Go to a football game, basketball game, or a hockey game and you will see it located somewhere near the playing field or ice. The device helps both the players and the fans know how much time is left in the game. What is it? A countdown clock.

Mark has been slowly notching up the tension in his Gospel. First, he told of how Jesus informed his disciples of his coming death. He then related how Jesus entered Jerusalem, the seat of power for the Jewish religious leaders who opposed him. Once in the city, Jesus proceeded to overturn the moneychangers' tables in the temple, engage in debates with the religious authorities, and predict the destruction of that same temple. All of this was in preparation of the final events that Mark will now relate in Jesus' ministry.

This "countdown clock" begins with Mark telling us the Passover was only two days away—and it will be ushered in with an unusual anointing in preparation of Jesus' burial. Jesus will be killed on the third day after this anointing and subsequent plot raised against him. Passover commemorated the liberation of Israel from Egypt, so this detail is important. The Messiah was about to bring another kind of deliverance . . . but not one people expected.

Jesus is Anointed [Mark 14:1–11]

[1] Now the Passover and the Festival of Unleavened Bread were only two days away, and the chief priests and the teachers of the law were scheming to arrest Jesus secretly and kill him. [2] "But not during the festival," they said, "or the people may riot."

[3] While he was in Bethany, reclining at the table in the home of Simon the Leper, a woman came with an alabaster jar of very expensive perfume, made of pure nard. She broke the jar and poured the perfume on his head.

[4] Some of those present were saying indignantly to one another, "Why this waste of perfume? [5] It could have been sold for more than a year's wages and the money given to the poor." And they rebuked her harshly.

[6] "Leave her alone," said Jesus. "Why are you bothering her? She has done a beautiful thing to me. [7] The poor you will always have with you, and you can help them any time you want. But you will not always have me. [8] She did what she could. She poured perfume on my body beforehand to prepare for my burial. [9] Truly I tell you, wherever the gospel is preached throughout the world, what she has done will also be told, in memory of her."

[10] Then Judas Iscariot, one of the Twelve, went to the chief priests to betray Jesus to them. [11] They were delighted to hear this and promised to give him money. So he watched for an opportunity to hand him over.

Original Meaning

During the Passover festival, thousands of pilgrims flocked to Jerusalem, creating headaches for the authorities. Passover commemorated the liberation of God's people from Egypt, when the Lord sent a plague that claimed the lives of the Egyptians' firstborn sons. The Israelites were "passed over" from this plague by dabbing the blood of a slaughtered lamb on their doorways. Many in Jesus' day saw this first deliverance as the model for their final liberation.

When this festival is two days away, Jesus dines in the home of Simon the Leper. Mark provides no details about this man or why Jesus is in his house. Rather, what Mark highlights for his readers is what happened there. A woman breaks into the company of men and pours precious perfume over Jesus' head. Again, we are given no information about this woman or why she does this. It could be that she is following a common custom of the day to show Jesus hospitality and honor. Or it could be that she believes she is anointing the Messiah (literally "the anointed one") with the oil of crowning to set him apart for his office.

Regardless of the woman's intent, Jesus declares that her actions have prepared him for burial. She has anointed not a king who will ascend a temporal throne and crush his mortal enemies but a king who is going to die for everyone—including those who view him as an enemy. Some contend she is the only follower of Jesus who understands the implications of his teaching. She knows he is destined to die and seizes this last opportunity to express her love. Meanwhile, Judas Iscariot sees this as an opportunity to betray his master.

❖ What was the nature of the bystanders' complaint against the woman? How did Jesus respond when they rebuked her harshly?

Past to Present

Consider what this passage meant to the original readers and how it applies to us today.

Extravagance Toward Jesus

It would have been hard for Mark's original readers to miss the stark contrast in attitudes between the woman in this story and the bystanders who witnessed the scene. The woman's extravagant devotion exuded devotion and love for Christ. Her gesture displayed the proper personal devotion a disciple should show to Jesus. Meanwhile, Judas Iscariot—one of the Twelve who was among those bystanders—will go on to show his lack of devotion by plotting with the chief priests.

The story prompts each of us to consider *how much is too much devotion to Jesus.* A little oil, as was customary for most Jewish anointings at the time, seems fine. But to break open a whole jar of expensive perfume just appears to be too extravagant. A little bit of devotion to Jesus—like serving at church on Sundays—seem fine and appropriate. But what if Jesus asks us to do something especially sacrificial for him? All who seek to be followers of Jesus need to examine their hearts and count the cost of what it means to be his disciple.

❖ Are there any limitations that you are putting on your acts of devotion to Jesus? If so, what do you need to do to release those limitations?

_____

_____

_____

_____

_____

_____

_____

❖ How would you describe the "cost" of being a disciple of Jesus? When are times that he has called you to make sacrifices for him?

_____

_____

_____

_____

Significance in God's Kingdom

There is another aspect of the woman's actions that we need to consider. While we do not know her exact motives for anointing Jesus, it is safe to assume she was not aware of how significant those actions would be in God's story of redemption. Jesus' commendation reveals that she was pouring perfume on his body to prepare him for burial—something she could not have known. Jesus added, "Truly I tell you, wherever the gospel is preached throughout the world, what she has done will also be told, in memory of her" (Mark 14:9).

God instructs us not to "despise the day of small things" (Zechariah 4:10). It is a mistake for us think our acts of sacrificial devotion—regardless of what form they might take—are ever wasteful or insignificant. We simply cannot know how God will use our actions and weave them into his greater purposes and plans. Our role is simply to follow his will and _act_. When we faithfully and sacrificially "sow the seeds" of our dedication and service, we can trust that our Lord will bring about an abundant harvest for his kingdom.

❖ When is a time you did your best to act with sacrificial devotion and Jesus used what you did to accomplish more than you imagined?

_____

_____

_____

❖ How important is it for you to see the results of what you "sow" for the Lord? Why do you think that God asks you to just trust him for the "harvest"?

_____

_____

_____

_____

_____

_____

The Passover [Mark 14:17–31]

¹⁷ When evening came, Jesus arrived with the Twelve. ¹⁸ While they were reclining at the table eating, he said, "Truly I tell you, one of you will betray me—one who is eating with me."

¹⁹ They were saddened, and one by one they said to him, "Surely you don't mean me?"

²⁰ "It is one of the Twelve," he replied, "one who dips bread into the bowl with me. ²¹ The Son of Man will go just as it is written about him. But woe to that man who betrays the Son of Man! It would be better for him if he had not been born."

²² While they were eating, Jesus took bread, and when he had given thanks, he broke it and gave it to his disciples, saying, "Take it; this is my body."

²³ Then he took a cup, and when he had given thanks, he gave it to them, and they all drank from it.

²⁴ "This is my blood of the covenant, which is poured out for many," he said to them. ²⁵ "Truly I tell you, I will not drink again from the fruit of the vine until that day when I drink it new in the kingdom of God."

²⁶ When they had sung a hymn, they went out to the Mount of Olives.

²⁷ "You will all fall away," Jesus told them, "for it is written:

"'I will strike the shepherd,
and the sheep will be scattered.'
[28] But after I have risen, I will go ahead of you into Galilee."

[29] Peter declared, "Even if all fall away, I will not."

[30] "Truly I tell you," Jesus answered, "today—yes, tonight—before the rooster crows twice you yourself will disown me three times."

[31] But Peter insisted emphatically, "Even if I have to die with you, I will never disown you." And all the others said the same.

Original Meaning

The scene that Mark depicts of the disciples sharing the Passover with Jesus is one of sorrow, worry, and confusion. Jesus begins the meal with an announcement that one of the Twelve will betray him. In that day, eating bread with someone barred a person from engaging in hostile acts toward that individual. Table fellowship had greater significance for Jews than simply a social gathering. Eating together was evidence of peace, trust, forgiveness, and brotherhood. It was a horrendous act to betray the one who had given you his or her bread.

Jesus' next act is to connect the elements of the Passover meal to his own coming suffering and death. He breaks the bread and distributes it to his disciples, telling that what has just happened to the bread will happen to him. The broken bread given to the disciples also symbolizes that his death and resurrection will benefit them. In many way, it serves as an acted-out parable of Jesus offering up his life for the many. When the disciples take bread again after Jesus' resurrection, they will remember they have bread of a most unusual nature.

Jesus then connects the wine to his blood. In the Old Testament, the blood of sacrificial animals was poured out by the priests on the altar as an offering to atone for the sins of the people. Jesus reveals that his death will be a new sacrifice offered to God . . . no more sacrificial victims need be killed. The disciples, in drinking the cup, were entering into a communion relationship with Jesus, to the point they would share his destiny. Blood was also used to seal or inaugurate a covenant. Jesus' sacrificial death would thus also be a covenant-making event that marked a new act of redemption and began a new relationship between God and the people.

After the meal ends, Jesus tells the disciples that they will all fall away. Peter denies that he will do such a thing. His emphatic declaration will play a part in an upcoming story.

❖ What did Jesus mean when he said that the bread represented his body? What did Jesus mean when he referred to the wine as "my blood of the covenant" (verse 24)?

_____

_____

_____

_____

_____

_____

_____

Past to Present

The Purpose of Communion

The purpose of the Passover meal was to put each generation of the Jewish people in touch with God's salvation in the exodus and make it a present reality of salvation in their lives. The purpose of the Lord's Supper is much the same in the lives of followers of Jesus. It is not a memorial of something past and gone but a reminder of what Jesus has done for us and continues to do in our lives. It invites us to contemplate our hearts—just as the disciples did in the upper room—and confess all the ways we are being saved despite our betrayal of Jesus.

❖ How do you typically approach Communion? What does this passage in Mark reveal should be happening in your heart and in your community when you partake of it?

_____

_____

_____

_____

_____

_____

❖ The psalmist wrote, "Search me, God, and know my heart" (Psalm 139:23). How often do you invite God to do this in your life?

_____

_____

_____

_____

_____

Gethsemane [Mark 14:32–50]

32 They went to a place called Gethsemane, and Jesus said to his disciples, "Sit here while I pray." 33 He took Peter, James and John along with him, and he began to be deeply distressed and troubled. 34 "My soul is overwhelmed with sorrow to the point of death," he said to them. "Stay here and keep watch."

35 Going a little farther, he fell to the ground and prayed that if possible the hour might pass from him. 36 "Abba, Father," he said, "everything is possible for you. Take this cup from me. Yet not what I will, but what you will."

37 Then he returned to his disciples and found them sleeping. "Simon," he said to Peter, "are you asleep? Couldn't you keep watch for one

hour? [38] Watch and pray so that you will not fall into temptation. The spirit is willing, but the flesh is weak."

[39] Once more he went away and prayed the same thing. [40] When he came back, he again found them sleeping, because their eyes were heavy. They did not know what to say to him.

[41] Returning the third time, he said to them, "Are you still sleeping and resting? Enough! The hour has come. Look, the Son of Man is delivered into the hands of sinners. [42] Rise! Let us go! Here comes my betrayer!"

[43] Just as he was speaking, Judas, one of the Twelve, appeared. With him was a crowd armed with swords and clubs, sent from the chief priests, the teachers of the law, and the elders.

[44] Now the betrayer had arranged a signal with them: "The one I kiss is the man; arrest him and lead him away under guard." [45] Going at once to Jesus, Judas said, "Rabbi!" and kissed him. [46] The men seized Jesus and arrested him. [47] Then one of those standing near drew his sword and struck the servant of the high priest, cutting off his ear.

[48] "Am I leading a rebellion," said Jesus, "that you have come out with swords and clubs to capture me? [49] Every day I was with you, teaching in the temple courts, and you did not arrest me. But the Scriptures must be fulfilled." [50] Then everyone deserted him and fled.

Original Meaning

Jesus retires after the Last Supper to a place on the Mount of Olives called Gethsemane. Once there, he separates Peter, James, and John from the rest of the group to go with him to pray. Peter has just boasted that he will stand firm with Jesus in his trials—even if they lead to death. James and John had promised they could be baptized with Jesus' baptism and drink his cup (see Mark 10:39). Jesus gives them a chance to back up their statements.

Even so, Jesus knows the three will be of no help to him now, so he goes off a little farther to pray alone. Jesus trusts completely in God as his Father and is completely obedient. He also confesses God's omnipotence to spare him from suffering. Might there be another way? Might he escape the horrifying cup? Jesus is only met with the silence of heaven. There is no reassuring voice from heaven. No dove descends. No ministering angels come to serve him. God has already spoken, and his Son must obey. Jesus acquiesces to his Father's will.

Jesus' agonizing lament and submission to God's will contrast sharply with the stupor of his three disciples, who fail to keep watch and pray with him. When Jesus returns to wake them a third time, he announces that "the hour has come" (verse 41). A misguided rabble, deputized by the temple officials, invades Gethsemane with swords and clubs. The sad performance of Jesus' disciples in this moment dominates this scene. Judas gives Jesus no sign their fellowship has been broken as he turns the Savior over to certain death with a warm gesture of love. The disciples have awakened sufficiently by this time to make their shameless getaway. The Son of Man is handed over in accordance with God's will as attested by Scripture.

❖ How do the actions of the disciples reveal they had no grasp on the seriousness of the moment? How did they act when they realized Jesus was about to be arrested?

_____

_____

_____

_____

Past to Present

Surrender to God

Jesus had already handed himself over to death when he acted and taught as he did in the temple. He had brought his proclamation of

God's reign to the seat of human power. Now he was moving from the one who *acted* to the one who was *acted upon*. As Jesus waited for the hour to come, he cried out to God to be spared from the ordeal of the cross, yet he accepted the will of his Father. In the same way, we can cry out to God to be spared from our own cross—but in the end, we also must choose to accept God's plan.

Jesus' familiarity with God—addressing him as "Abba," the equivalent of our "Daddy"—allowed him to be honest about his fears and honest with God about what the plan required of him. Jesus did not try to run counter to the Father's purpose but explored the limits of that purpose without trying to burst its bounds. Jesus models for us what it means to *watch* and *wait*. He teaches us how to handle our own pain and suffering during such times. He instructs us on how to surrender our will to the Lord in every situation so we can participate in God's plans.

❖ What are some times in your life when you cried out to God much as Jesus did in this story? How did you sense God speaking to you in that moment?

_____

_____

_____

_____

❖ What is your biggest struggle when it comes to submitting your will to God? How has the Lord helped you in learning how to submit to him?

_____

_____

_____

_____

Remain Spiritually Awake

Peter, James, and John serve as negative examples in this story because they did not understand the critical importance of the moment and fell asleep while Jesus prayed. In our lives, we also succumb to such spiritual drowsiness when we fail to pray during our times of trial. Adversity brings out the worst in us while requiring the most of us. The only way we can ready ourselves to bear up under pressure is through fervent prayer.

We also fall victim to spiritual drowsiness when we do not recognize the onset of trials or accept them as part of God's will. The disciples heard only what they wanted to hear. They tuned out Jesus' words on the necessity of suffering or the requirement of taking up a cross—as evidenced by the fact they were able to drift off to sleep in Gethsemane. Meanwhile, Jesus was wide awake to the situation and seeking God in prayer.

Another way we can fall prey to spiritual drowsiness is to not be aware of our human weaknesses and limitations. In a parallel account of this story, Jesus said to his disciples, "The spirit is willing, but the flesh is weak" (Matthew 26:41). Jesus understood they lacked the strength for the spiritual battle that was to come, which is why he asked them to pray for divine strength. We must be ever mindful of our human frailty. As Paul wrote, "So, if you think you are standing firm, be careful that you don't fall!" (1 Corinthians 10:12).

❖ How has a regular practice of prayer and communion with God helped you to remain spiritually awake? How has this helped you when the spiritual battles have come?

_____

_____

_____

_____

_____

❖ When has pride or your inability to admit weakness led to a fall?
What did God teach you through that experience?

_____

_____

_____

_____

_____

_____

_____

_____

_____

Closing Prayer: *God of wisdom, thank you for loving me enough to give me clear and relevant warnings in your Word. Grant me wisdom to listen, comprehend, and follow your direction each day of my life. Help me to live and walk each day with confident faith that your Holy Spirit is leading me every step of the journey. Empower me to stay spiritually awake. Amen.*

The Mission Continues

Mark 14:53–72; 15:1–20, 21–47; 16:1–8

Writers today understand the importance of not only having a good *beginning* but also an appropriate *ending* to their stories. As readers, we want to know where all the drama and plot points in the story have been leading. By the time we reach the final sentence, we want to comprehend what the author intends us to take away from the overall account.

Mark began his Gospel with God's messenger (the prophet Isaiah) announcing what the Lord was about to do (see 1:2–8). Mark will now close his Gospel with another messenger (an angel) declaring what the Lord has done (see 16:6–7). In between, Jesus has been constantly on the move . . . and nothing changes as the story comes to an end. Jesus is not in the tomb for the women to cling to and embrace. Mark does not end his account with a joyful reunion. In fact, in the earliest and most reliable manuscripts, the Gospel ends with these two sentences: "Trembling and bewildered, the women went out and fled from the tomb. They said nothing to anyone, because they were afraid" (16:8). Such an ending seems too abrupt to us.

The question is . . . *why*? Why does Mark leave out the details of what happened after Jesus' resurrection that the other Gospel writers include? Much as how we needed to consider why Mark left out details regarding Jesus' backstory at the start of his Gospel, so we now need to consider why he ends his Gospel in this way. For, once again, he has a purpose in doing so.

Jesus Before the Religious Leaders [Mark 14:53–72]

53 They took Jesus to the high priest, and all the chief priests, the elders and the teachers of the law came together.

54 Peter followed him at a distance, right into the courtyard of the high priest. There he sat with the guards and warmed himself at the fire.

55 The chief priests and the whole Sanhedrin were looking for evidence against Jesus so that they could put him to death, but they did not find any. 56 Many testified falsely against him, but their statements did not agree.

57 Then some stood up and gave this false testimony against him: 58 "We heard him say, 'I will destroy this temple made with human hands and in three days will build another, not made with hands.'" 59 Yet even then their testimony did not agree.

60 Then the high priest stood up before them and asked Jesus, "Are you not going to answer? What is this testimony that these men are bringing against you?" 61 But Jesus remained silent and gave no answer.

Again the high priest asked him, "Are you the Messiah, the Son of the Blessed One?"

62 "I am," said Jesus. "And you will see the Son of Man sitting at the right hand of the Mighty One and coming on the clouds of heaven."

63 The high priest tore his clothes. "Why do we need any more witnesses?" he asked. 64 "You have heard the blasphemy. What do you think?"

They all condemned him as worthy of death. 65 Then some began to spit at him; they blindfolded him, struck him with their fists, and said, "Prophesy!" And the guards took him and beat him.

66 While Peter was below in the courtyard, one of the servant girls of the high priest came by. 67 When she saw Peter warming himself, she looked closely at him.

"You also were with that Nazarene, Jesus," she said.

[68] But he denied it. "I don't know or understand what you're talking about," he said, and went out into the entryway.

[69] When the servant girl saw him there, she said again to those standing around, "This fellow is one of them." [70] Again he denied it.

After a little while, those standing near said to Peter, "Surely you are one of them, for you are a Galilean."

[71] He began to call down curses, and he swore to them, "I don't know this man you're talking about."

[72] Immediately the rooster crowed the second time. Then Peter remembered the word Jesus had spoken to him: "Before the rooster crows twice you will disown me three times." And he broke down and wept.

Original Meaning

Mark's readers would have seen in this story that it is the high priest and his Sanhedrin who take the primary responsibility and initiative for Jesus' death. Although Mark writes "all the chief priests" have gathered (verse 53), this doesn't mean all seventy-one members of the Sanhedrin (as dictated by later rabbinic tradition) are present. More likely, this group consists of whatever members can be gathered at the late hour. Mark's readers would have understood that holding a trial in the middle of the night indicates that a sort of kangaroo court was taking place. It also shows these leaders were under time constraints.

Jewish law only allowed the condemnation of an accused person based on the evidence of two or more witnesses who agreed (see Deuteronomy 19:15–21). Mark notes the witnesses giving testimony against Jesus do *not* agree—and Jesus remains silent in the face of their accusations. Finally, the high priest takes charge and asks Jesus directly, "Are you the Messiah, the Son of the Blessed One?" (Mark 14:61). Jesus publicly accepts that he is the Messiah with his reply: "I am." He then publicly affirms his identity before the high priest and his council with this statement: "And you will see the Son of Man sitting at the right hand of the Mighty One and coming on the clouds of heaven" (verse 62). To the high priest, the evidence is conclusive. Jesus has incriminated himself. The council unanimously declares him worthy of death.

While all this is taking place, Peter is waiting outside in the courtyard. His trial there can be seen as a parody of his Lord's. While Jesus is under fire inside, Peter warms himself by the fire outside. As Jesus confesses under immense pressure and seals his fate, Peter capitulates under the gentlest of pressure and lies to save himself. He swears an oath that he does not even know Jesus. All of this happens just as Jesus said it would (see 14:29–30).

❖ How does Jesus respond when the witnesses present false testimony against him? Why did his statement to the high priest seal his fate?

_____

_____

_____

Past to Present

Consider what this passage meant to the original readers and how it applies to us today.

The Son of Man
Jesus says in his answer to the chief priest that he is the "Son of Man" (verse 62). This title appears in Daniel 7:13 to refer to an enigmatic figure associated with power, glory, heavenly exaltation, and judgment. This figure is also seen as being distinct from the righteous community in that he does not suffer what the community does. However, in Mark's Gospel we see the Son of Man associated with power that blends and requires both suffering and weakness.

Such a concept would have required Mark's Jewish readers to completely rethink what they believed about the Messiah and their expectations of power. Jesus as the Messiah was *less* than people hoped, because he did not seek political power and submitted to his death. Yet Jesus as the Messiah was *greater* than anyone hoped, because he divinely exercised the power of God. Just like Mark's readers, we need to examine our expectations of how and where we will see God's power at work in our world. As Paul wrote, "But [God] said to me, 'My grace is sufficient for you, for my power is made perfect in weakness.' Therefore I will boast all the more gladly about my weaknesses, so that Christ's power may rest on me" (2 Corinthians 12:9).

❖ What assumptions and expectations about Jesus have you held that are challenged by your reading of Mark's Gospel?

_____

_____

_____

_____

❖ What are some of the ways that you have seen God's power at work in your world?

_____

_____

_____

_____

The God of Second Chances

Three times, Peter failed to understand Jesus' announcement of his suffering. Three times, he did not heed Jesus' appeal to watch, stay awake, and pray. When the time of trial came, he then three times denied knowing Jesus. Peter relied on his own strength—and failed—yet we can find solace in the account of his denials. He was the most prominent of Jesus' disciples, yet he was still a sinner in need of God's mercy. He was confident that he would die for Jesus, but he needed Jesus to die for him. Peter needed a second chance—just as we do.

If Peter could be restored after denying his Lord (and even cursing him), then there is hope for anyone who is guilty of the same (or worse). Jesus says to each of us: "It is not the healthy who need a doctor, but the sick. I have not come to call the righteous, but sinners" (Mark 2:17). Given that "all have sinned and fall short of the glory of God" (Romans 3:23), we *all* need healing from Jesus. We *all* are sinners who have fallen short of God's glory and need Jesus to restore us to righteousness. And we *all* receive these kinds of second chances (and even beyond) from Jesus, who says to us, "Your sins are forgiven" (Mark 2:5).

❖ How does the story of Peter's public denial of Jesus provide you with hope today?

_____

_____

_____

_____

_____

❖ In what ways are you in need of a "second chance" from God today?

_____

_____

_____

_____

_____

_____

Jesus Before Pilate [Mark 15:1–20]

[1] Very early in the morning, the chief priests, with the elders, the teachers of the law and the whole Sanhedrin, made their plans. So they bound Jesus, led him away and handed him over to Pilate.

[2] "Are you the king of the Jews?" asked Pilate.

"You have said so," Jesus replied.

[3] The chief priests accused him of many things. [4] So again Pilate asked him, "Aren't you going to answer? See how many things they are accusing you of."

[5] But Jesus still made no reply, and Pilate was amazed.

[6] Now it was the custom at the festival to release a prisoner whom the people requested. [7] A man called Barabbas was in prison with the insurrectionists who had committed murder in the uprising. [8] The crowd came up and asked Pilate to do for them what he usually did.

[9] "Do you want me to release to you the king of the Jews?" asked Pilate, [10] knowing it was out of self-interest that the chief priests had handed Jesus over to him. [11] But the chief priests stirred up the crowd to have Pilate release Barabbas instead.

[12] "What shall I do, then, with the one you call the king of the Jews?" Pilate asked them.

[13] "Crucify him!" they shouted.

[14] "Why? What crime has he committed?" asked Pilate.

But they shouted all the louder, "Crucify him!"

[15] Wanting to satisfy the crowd, Pilate released Barabbas to them. He had Jesus flogged, and handed him over to be crucified.

[16] The soldiers led Jesus away into the palace (that is, the Praetorium) and called together the whole company of soldiers. [17] They put a purple robe on him, then twisted together a crown of thorns and set it on him. [18] And they began to call out to him, "Hail, king of the Jews!" [19] Again and again they struck him on the head with a staff and spit on him. Falling on their knees, they paid homage to him. [20] And when they had mocked

him, they took off the purple robe and put his own clothes on him. Then they led him out to crucify him.

Original Meaning

The action now moves from the chamber of the Sanhedrin to the court of the Roman governor Pontius Pilate—the true political authority in the land. The Romans did not interfere in local politics any more than was necessary to maintain order. A large part of Pilate's everyday chores of governance and administration thus fell to the local councils and magistrates. They had the power to arrest, take evidence, and make preliminary examination for the purpose of presenting a prosecution case before the governor for a formal trial.

The Jewish religious authorities knew that Pilate would not condemn Jesus to death simply for violating Jewish religious regulations. Such religious matters did not concern Roman governors—provided they did not become political matters. For this reason, the Jewish leaders had to reformulate their charge against Jesus in a way that would force Pilate to take it seriously. Given that Pilate's first question to Jesus is, "Are you the king of the Jews?" (verse 2), it is likely that this is the charge the Jewish leaders made against him. If Jesus claimed to be a king, they reasoned, he was guilty of a crime committed against the power of Rome.

Pilate had evidently chosen to release a prisoner once a year to appease the people. However, when he offers up Jesus to be set free, the crowd clamors for the release of the murderous Barabbas. Mark only tells us "the chief priests stirred up the crowd" (verse 11), and since Pilate wanted "to satisfy the crowd" (verse 15), he gave them their victim. Mark reports that Jesus is flogged and the whole company of soldiers (around six hundred) joins in the mockery of Jesus. They deck him out in royal purple and twist together a crown of thorns. They hail him as "king of the Jews" (verse 18) and mockingly bow down before him.

❖ How would you describe Pilate's attitude toward the charges the chief priests brought against Jesus? What compelled him to ultimately sentence Jesus to death?

_____

_____

_____

_____

_____

Past to Present

Pleasing the Crowd

Even early on in Christian tradition, Pilate came off as a rather sympathetic figure. He seems to be almost helpless in this story as he looks at the crowd demanding Jesus' execution and asks, "What shall I do . . . ?" (verse 12). It is almost as if he is shaking his head as he cedes responsibility and agrees to the injustice taking place. Pilate is the type of leader who forever has his finger in the wind to see which way it is blowing and does something for others as long as it costs him nothing. He will not pursue truth or justice. He only wants to satisfy the crowd, whose intentions he knows are less than honorable, and allows them to make his decisions.

As followers of Jesus, it can be hard for us to admit that we have tendencies like Pilate. We, too, have our finger in the wind to see which way the popular opinion is blowing. We, too, often choose to do something for others only if it costs us nothing. We, too, fail to pursue truth or justice if it means sacrifice or a hit on our reputation. We forget this warning from James: "Do not merely listen to the word, and so deceive yourselves. Do what it says" (1:22). Rather than sit back like Pilate and let injustice play out, our heavenly Father says, "Defend the weak and the fatherless; uphold the cause of the poor and the oppressed" (Psalm 82:3).

❖ What traits of Pilate in this story do you observe in your life?

_____

_____

_____

_____

❖ When is a time you stood up for injustice in your world? What happened as a result?

_____

_____

_____

_____

Following the Crowd

Barabbas may have been a right-wing extremist fighting to deliver Israel from the pollution of Roman rule, or he may have simply been a bandit whose victims were typically the rich landlords and their retainers. The common people, from whose ranks the bandits came, often looked to them as heroic figures who exacted vengeance against their oppressors. Given this, Barabbas may have been a hero in their eyes, which explains their choice to set him free.

The choice of Barabbas represents the human preference for the one who represents our narrow personal hopes—in this particular case, a perverted nationalism. As followers of Jesus, it can be difficult to admit that we sometimes also hail what Barabbas represents and call for what Jesus represents to be crucified. We choose the never-ending cycle of violence of Barabbas and reject the love, forgiveness, and active stand against injustice and oppression of Jesus. Sadly, the truth is that while we trust God to take care of the afterlife, we do not always trust him enough to let go of our control of the here and now.

❖ What does "Barabbas" represent in your world today? Why is his way often more compelling than following the way of Jesus?

_____

_____

_____

_____

❖ In what areas of your life do you sense you need to trust God more? What do you think God could accomplish if you surrendered those areas to him?

_____

_____

_____

_____

Crucifixion, Death, and Burial [Mark 15:21–47]

21 A certain man from Cyrene, Simon, the father of Alexander and Rufus, was passing by on his way in from the country, and they forced him to carry the cross. 22 They brought Jesus to the place called Golgotha (which means "the place of the skull"). 23 Then they offered him wine mixed with myrrh, but he did not take it. 24 And they crucified him. Dividing up his clothes, they cast lots to see what each would get.

25 It was nine in the morning when they crucified him. 26 The written notice of the charge against him read: THE KING OF THE JEWS.

27 They crucified two rebels with him, one on his right and one on his left. [28] 29 Those who passed by hurled insults at him, shaking their heads and saying, "So! You who are going to destroy the temple and build it in three days, 30 come down from the cross and save yourself!" 31 In the same way the chief priests and the teachers of the law mocked him

among themselves. "He saved others," they said, "but he can't save himself! ³² Let this Messiah, this king of Israel, come down now from the cross, that we may see and believe." Those crucified with him also heaped insults on him.

³³ At noon, darkness came over the whole land until three in the afternoon. ³⁴ And at three in the afternoon Jesus cried out in a loud voice, "Eloi, Eloi, lema sabachthani?" (which means "My God, my God, why have you forsaken me?").

³⁵ When some of those standing near heard this, they said, "Listen, he's calling Elijah."

³⁶ Someone ran, filled a sponge with wine vinegar, put it on a staff, and offered it to Jesus to drink. "Now leave him alone. Let's see if Elijah comes to take him down," he said.

³⁷ With a loud cry, Jesus breathed his last.

³⁸ The curtain of the temple was torn in two from top to bottom. ³⁹ And when the centurion, who stood there in front of Jesus, saw how he died, he said, "Surely this man was the Son of God!"

⁴⁰ Some women were watching from a distance. Among them were Mary Magdalene, Mary the mother of James the younger and of Joseph, and Salome. ⁴¹ In Galilee these women had followed him and cared for his needs. Many other women who had come up with him to Jerusalem were also there.

⁴² It was Preparation Day (that is, the day before the Sabbath). So as evening approached, ⁴³ Joseph of Arimathea, a prominent member of the Council, who was himself waiting for the kingdom of God, went boldly to Pilate and asked for Jesus' body. ⁴⁴ Pilate was surprised to hear that he was already dead. Summoning the centurion, he asked him if Jesus had already died. ⁴⁵ When he learned from the centurion that it was so, he gave the body to Joseph. ⁴⁶ So Joseph bought some linen cloth, took down the body, wrapped it in the linen, and placed it in a tomb cut out of rock. Then he rolled a stone against the entrance of the tomb. ⁴⁷ Mary Magdalene and Mary the mother of Joseph saw where he was laid.

Original Meaning

Mark identifies the man who carried Jesus' cross as Simon from Cyrene in North Africa. Most likely, Mark includes the names of his sons, Alexander and Rufus, because they were known to early Christians. Jesus is brought to Golgotha, which Mark interprets as "the place of the skull." The name could refer to an outcropping of rock that resembled a skull, the discovery of a skull (or skulls) in this place, or the fact that it was a site for executions.

Jesus is crucified at nine o'clock in the morning. At noon, a darkness comes over the land that lasts until the death of Jesus at three o'clock in the afternoon. Jesus' cry from the cross, "My God, my God, why have you forsaken me," comes from Psalm 22:1—a lament that ends with a triumphant hope of vindication. Jesus' death establishes the sovereignty of God, who has sent his beloved Son to give his life as a ransom for many (see Mark 10:45).

Mark reports that the veil in the temple rips from top to bottom at Jesus' death. The scene is reminiscent of the story of Jesus' baptism at the beginning of the Gospel (see Mark 1:9–11). When Jesus ascended from the waters at his baptism, he saw the heavens being torn open, representing the breaking of God's kingdom into the world. Now, the veil in the temple, which screened the Holy Place from the Most Holy Place, is torn into two pieces. For the first time, all human beings can fully see what God intends to reveal.

Mark reveals that a group of grieving women have followed Jesus from Galilee and look on at the execution from a distance. Unlike the disciples, they have not vanished from the scene. A man named Joseph "of Arimathea" then takes the initiative in securing Jesus' body for burial. Pilate's concern is to make sure Jesus is already dead, which is confirmed by a centurion who has just confessed that Jesus is the Son of God. Pilate's quick granting of Joseph's request confirms that he did not seriously consider Jesus guilty of treason.

❖ What were some of the insults the passersby hurled at Jesus? What does this indicate about their disappointment in Jesus not being what they expected in a Messiah?

_____

_____

_____

_____

Past to Present

Lessons from the Cross

Mark's concise and sober picture of Jesus on the cross indicates that something more profound was happening than just another Roman execution. The cross has deep significance. It is the point at which the blind rage of humanity against God was unleashed with a horrible intensity. At the cross, both the religious and irreligious inflicted their wounds on the heart of God.

In our lives, the cross reveals several profound truths to us today. First, it reveals *God's staggering power* to confront the wages of human sin and decisively provide salvation for all who put their trust in Jesus. The cross reveals that God has indeed witnessed the violence inflicted there on Jesus and uses it to save the world from itself. Second, the cross *reveals God's incredible love*. We see who God truly is when we witness the Son of God crying out from the cross and then raised in glory.

Third, the cross reveals that *things are never what they seem* in our world. It may seem to us at times as if God is absent. But he remains firmly in control and accomplishes his purposes. Fourth, it reveals that *God's love and power can win those whom we never dreamed would respond*. The words of the centurion who put Jesus to death and the actions of Joseph, a respected and wealthy member of the council that condemned Jesus to death, mean that one can never write off an enemy. The gospel has the power to change all people.

Fifth, the cross *reveals the pain of the human situation.* The Son of God took on our humanity and embraced all the bitter suffering and anguish of the world. Defeat may tempt us to give up our faith, but Jesus' cry on the cross reveals a faith that will not let go of God even when deluged by the greatest of all suffering. Finally, the cross *reveals a new way of life.* Jesus' death shows that he lived out his teachings. The one who tries to save their life will lose it, but the one who gives up their life will gain it and will give life to others.

❖ How has the cross of Jesus revealed the love of God toward you? In what ways is Jesus showing you this love today?

The Resurrection [Mark 16:1–8]

¹When the Sabbath was over, Mary Magdalene, Mary the mother of James, and Salome bought spices so that they might go to anoint Jesus' body. ² Very early on the first day of the week, just after sunrise, they were on their way to the tomb ³ and they asked each other, "Who will roll the stone away from the entrance of the tomb?"

⁴ But when they looked up, they saw that the very large stone had been rolled away. ⁵ As they entered the tomb, they saw a young man dressed in a white robe sitting on the right side, and they were alarmed.

⁶ "Don't be alarmed," he said. "You are looking for Jesus the Nazarene, who was crucified. He has risen! He is not here. See the place where they laid him. ⁷ But go, tell his disciples and Peter, 'He is going ahead of you into Galilee. There you will see him, just as he told you.'"

⁸ Trembling and bewildered, the women went out and fled from the tomb. They said nothing to anyone, because they were afraid.

Conclusion

We now come to the conclusion of what most scholars believe to be the end of Mark's Gospel. The group of grieving women at the cross arrive at the tomb and find the stone rolled away. An angel informs them that Jesus has risen and gone ahead to Galilee. The women flee from the tomb and say nothing to anyone—leaving us to fill in what happens next. What we discover is that the resurrection is only the beginning of the gospel that must be proclaimed throughout the world. The women certainly did tell the disciples that Jesus had risen, and they did go into Galilee, and there they saw Jesus. But now, the command is for them to *tell something about him*. There is no need for silence or secrets. Jesus now commands an open proclamation that he is indeed the Messiah!

❖ What surprises you the most about Mark's ending to this story? What is your greatest takeaway after studying the entire Gospel?

_____

_____

_____

_____

❖ What are you doing to *tell something about Jesus* to those who need the gospel in your world? How are you partnering with God in this?

_____

_____

_____

_____

Closing Prayer: Lord, breathe new life into my soul. Help me walk in the hope, grace, and power of your resurrection. May your sacrifice remind me to lay down my life, take up your cross, and walk in the newness of life that is found in you. Give me the words to share the gospel with others. Amen!

About

KEVIN HARNEY and DAVID E. GARLAND

Dr. Kevin G. Harney is the president and co-founder of Organic Outreach International and the teaching pastor of Shoreline Church in Monterey, California. He is the author of the *Organic Outreach* trilogy, *Organic Disciples*, more than one hundred small group guides, and numerous articles. He does extensive teaching and speaking nationally and internationally to equip leaders in effective and culture-changing discipleship and evangelism. He and his wife, Sherry, have three married sons, three daughters-in-law, and five grandchildren.

David E. Garland (PhD, Southern Baptist Theological Seminary) is professor emeritus of Christian Scriptures George W. Truett Seminary, Baylor University. He is the author of *A Theology of Mark's Gospel* and has written commentaries on each of the Synoptic Gospels, Acts, Romans, both Corinthian epistles, Colossians, and Philemon. He also served as the New Testament editor for the revised Expositor's Bible Commentary.

ALSO AVAILABLE

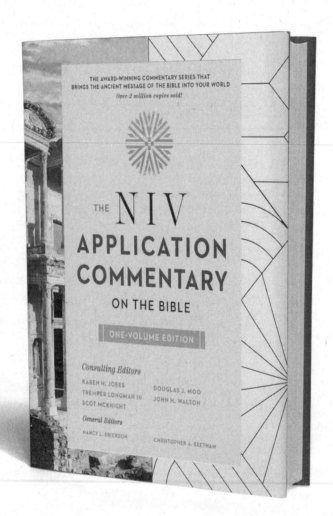

AVAILABLE WHEREVER BOOKS ARE SOLD